Study Guide

for

Slavin
Educational Psychology
Theory and Practice
Sixth Edition

Catherine E. McCartney
Bemidji State University

Allyn and Bacon
Boston London Toronto Sydney Tokyo Singapore

Study Guide

for

Educational Psychology
Theory and Practice
Sixth Edition

CONTENTS

TO THE STUDENT

Chapter 1
EDUCATIONAL PSYCHOLOGY: A FOUNDATION FOR TEACHING   1

Chapter 2
THEORIES OF DEVELOPMENT   13

Chapter 3
DEVELOPMENT DURING CHILDHOOD AND ADOLESCENCE   33

Chapter 4
STUDENT DIVERSITY   49

Chapter 5
BEHAVIORAL THEORIES OF LEARNING   69

Chapter 6
COGNITIVE THEORIES OF LEARNING: BASIC CONCEPTS   83

Chapter 7
THE EFFECTIVE LESSON   102

Chapter 8
STUDENT CENTERED AND CONSTRUCTIVIST APPROACHES   115

Chapter 9
ACCOMMODATING INSTRUCTION TO MEET INDIVIDUAL NEEDS   124

Chapter 10
MOTIVATING STUDENTS TO LEARN   141

Chapter 11
EFFECTIVE LEARNING ENVIRONMENTS   154

Chapter 12
EXCEPTIONAL LEARNERS   169

Chapter 13
ASSESSING STUDENT LEARNING   181

Chapter 14
STANDARDIZED TESTS AND GRADES   194

TO THE STUDENT

PURPOSE OF THE STUDY GUIDE

The purpose of this study guide is to reinforce your understanding of the information presented in the text *Educational Psychology: Theory and Practice* by Robert E. Slavin. Both the text and the guide are organized by chapter headings, which are questions focusing on what you should know after you complete your study of the chapters. If you preview the headings for each chapter, study the related text material, and assess your understanding of the content by using this study guide, you should have a firm grasp of the concepts, principles, and theories that make up the field of educational psychology.

ORGANIZATION OF THE CHAPTERS IN THE STUDY GUIDE

CHAPTER OVERVIEW | A brief overview of the concepts presented in the chapter, along with an explanation of how the chapter fits into the rest of the text, is included in this section.

CHAPTER OUTLINE | Chapter headings and subheadings from the text that identify important questions to be answered while reading guide the organization of the outline.

PRACTICE TEST | A series of five to ten questions, worth a total of ten points, is included in this section to assess your understanding of the chapter information. Mastery of the material is reached when you score nine points. Answers to the questions are provided at the end of each chapter.

FOR YOUR INFORMATION | In this section, further study, focusing on the self-check items from the text, is provided if the practice test questions reveal that you have not yet mastered the information.

FOR YOUR ENJOYMENT | In this section, suggestions for enriching your knowledge of chapter information are included.

SELF-ASSESSMENT | This section includes multiple choice, matching, and short essay items covering the main ideas in each chapter. Answers to the questions are included at the end of the study guide.

HOW TO USE THE STUDY GUIDE

1. Preview the headings identified in the text chapter.

2. Read the text chapter while paying close attention to the headings and subheadings.

3. Turn to the *Study Guide* and read the CHAPTER OVERVIEW and the CHAPTER OUTLINE. The points in each should be familiar since they are closely integrated with the text.

4. Recite what you remember from your reading. Use the FOR YOUR ENJOYMENT SECTION to find enrichment, research, or term paper ideas.

5. Use the PRACTICE TEST section to assess your knowledge of the material. If you score less than nine out of ten points, turn to the FOR YOUR INFORMATION section for further study, then complete the SELF-ASSESSMENT items.

1
EDUCATIONAL PSYCHOLOGY: A FOUNDATION FOR TEACHING

CHAPTER OVERVIEW

The purpose of this chapter is to provide you with a foundation for understanding effective teaching by using research from the field of educational psychology. Some of the things already learned from studies in educational psychology are listed below.

Educational psychology describes good teachers as those who possess subject matter knowledge and pedagogical knowledge (teaching "know how") that they combine with common sense to make sound decisions about classroom events.

Educational psychology teaches us that good teachers are intentional teachers, which means they do things for a reason, on purpose.

Educational psychology has taught us that good teachers use quantitative and qualitative research findings that describe teaching effectiveness to guide their instruction.

CHAPTER OUTLINE

I. WHAT MAKES A GOOD TEACHER?
    A. Knowing the Subject Matters
    B. Mastering the Teaching Skills
    C. Can Good Teaching be Taught?
    D. The Intentional Teacher

II. WHAT IS THE ROLE OF RESEARCH IN EDUCATIONAL PSYCHOLOGY?
    A. Goals of Research in Educational Psychology ‘
    B. The Value of Research in Educational Psychology to the Teacher
    C. Teaching as Decision Making
    D. Research + Common Sense = Effective Teaching
    E. Research on Effective Programs
    F. Impact of Research on Educational Practice

III. WHAT RESEARCH METHODS ARE USED IN EDUCATIONAL PSYCHOLOGY?
    A. Experiments
    B. Correlational Studies
    C. Descriptive Research

PRACTICE TEST

DIRECTIONS: Each chapter heading from the text listed below is followed by a series of related questions worth a total of ten points. Respond to each question, check your answers with those found at the end of the study guide chapter, then determine your score. Consider nine points per heading to be mastery.

For those headings on which you do not score at least nine points, turn to the FOR YOUR INFORMATION section of the study guide for corrective instruction. For those headings on which you do score at least nine points, turn to the FOR YOUR ENJOYMENT section of the study guide for enrichment activities.

I. WHAT MAKES A GOOD TEACHER?

True or False

1. (1 point) _____ According to your text author, personal characteristics such as leadership, humor, and enthusiasm are only part of what makes someone an effective teacher.

2. (1 point) _____ Effective teaching is a matter of one person with more knowledge transmitting that knowledge to someone with less.

3. (1 point) _____ The connection between what the teacher wants students to know and what the students actually learn is called pedagogy.

Multiple Choice

4. (1 point) _____ Teachers who continually experiment with strategies to solve problems of instruction and then observe the results of their actions to see if they were effective possess which of the following attributes?

   A. subject matter knowledge
   B. intentionality
   C. charisma
   D. momentum

5. (1 point) _____ Teachers who constantly upgrade and examine their teaching practices, read and attend conferences to learn new ideas, and use their students' responses to guide their instruction are

   A. tenured teachers.
   B. critical thinkers.
   C. members of a teachers' union.
   D. experienced teachers.

Short Answer/Essay

6. (2 points) Explain how good teaching can be taught.

_____

_____

7. (3 points) Describe an intentional teacher.

_____

_____

_____

2

II. WHAT IS THE ROLE OF RESEARCH IN EDUCATIONAL PSYCHOLOGY?

8. (1 point) _____

True or False
A goal of educational psychology research is to carefully examine questions about teaching and learning using objective methods.

9. (1 point) _____

Principles and theories from educational psychology research are interpreted in similar ways by different individuals, making progress in the field steady and evenly paced.

10. (3 points)

Matching

_____ set of related relationships that explain broad aspects of an area of study

_____ ideas that have been thoroughly tested and found to apply to a wide variety of situations

_____ an explanation of the relationship between factors

A. laws

B. principles

C. theories

11. (1 point) _____

Multiple choice
Which of the following ideas about teaching can be supported by educational psychology research?

A. Schools that spend more money per pupil will produce higher achieving students than schools that spend less.
B. If students are assigned to classes according to their ability, the resulting narrow range of abilities in a class will let the teacher adapt the instruction to the students' needs, resulting in higher achievement.
C. Scolding students in order to improve behavior may work for many, but for some it is a reward.
D. Competition among students, not cooperation, is most effective in terms of achievement.

12. (1 point) _____

When you combine objective research with common sense, the result is

A. effective teaching.
B. a cause and effect relationship.
C. inconsistent student achievement.
D. decreased quality in decision making.

13. (1 point) _____ Which of the following statements regarding teacher decision making is false?

A. Sound decision making depends on the situation within which a problem arises.
B. Sound decision making depends on the objectives the teacher has in mind.
C. It is necessary to combine principles and theories from educational psychology with common sense when making decisions.
D. Principles and theories from educational psychology can be considered free of context.

Short Answer/Essay

14. (2 points)   Explain how educational research affects educational practice.

_____

_____

III. WHAT RESEARCH METHODS ARE USED IN EDUCATIONAL PSYCHOLOGY?

15. (3 points)

Matching

_____ examples of this type of research include surveys, interviews, or observations, which take place in a social setting

A. experimental

B. correlational

C. descriptive

_____ type of research where special treatments are created and their effects analyzed

_____ type of research where relationships between variables, as they naturally occur, are analyzed

Multiple Choice

16. (1 point) _____ One advantage to this type of experimental research is that there is a high degree of control over all factors involved. One disadvantage is that the artificial conditions under which the experiment is conducted may yield results that have little real-life relevance. What type of research is being described in the above statements?

A. laboratory experiment
B. randomized-field experiment
C. single-case experiment

17. (1 point) _____ A special education teacher collects data on the number of times a student's hand-raising behavior occurs over a period of several days after a new assertiveness program has been implemented. What type of research is being described?

A. laboratory experiment
B. randomized-field experiment
C. single-case experiment

18. (1 point) _____ Which of the following experimental research types attempts to control all factors except those created by the treatment while simultaneously remaining relevant to real life?

A. laboratory experiment
B. randomized-field experiment
C. single-case experiment

19. (1 point) _____ A researcher found that students who scored high on a test of reading achievement also scored high on a self-esteem inventory. This means that reading achievement and self-esteem are

A. negatively correlated.
B. positively correlated.
C. unrelated.

20. (1 point) _____ Which of the following examples depicts a negative correlation?

A. Students who studied for the greatest length of time prior to a math test received the highest scores.
B. The amount of time students studied for a math test was unrelated to the scores they received.
C. Students who were absent the least prior to a math test received the highest scores. '

21. (2 points)

Short Answer/Essay
Explain the difference between causal and correlation relationships.

_____

_____

SCORING	POINTS NEEDED FOR MASTERY	POINTS RECEIVED
I. WHAT MAKES A GOOD TEACHER?	9	_____
II. WHAT IS THE ROLE OF RESEARCH IN EDUCATIONAL PSYCHOLOGY?	9	_____
III. WHAT RESEARCH METHODS ARE USED IN EDUCATIONAL PSYCHOLOGY?	9	_____

5

FOR YOUR INFORMATION

This section of the study guide includes suggestions for further study of the information you have not yet mastered. You will find information on: 1) typical responses to the SELF-CHECK item(s) from the text; and 2) key concepts, principles, and theories addressed in the text chapter.

I. WHAT MAKES A GOOD TEACHER?

1. SELF-CHECK ITEM: Reassess the chapter opening scenario. In terms of concepts introduced in this section, what qualities identify Leah as an intentional teacher?

TYPICAL RESPONSE: What qualities identify Leah as an intentional teacher?

Qualities of an Intentional Teacher	Qualities of Leah Washington
motivates students	Leah says "I read students funny and intriguing stories . . . to arouse their curiosity."
assesses prior knowledge	Leah says "I adapt to the needs of each learner by conferencing with students and helping them with specific problems."
communicates effectively	Leah "gradually introduced 'mini-lessons' to help [students] become better authors."
takes into account the characteristics of the learner	Leah says "I adapt to students' developmental levels and cultural styles by encouraging them to write about things that matter to them."
assesses learning outcomes	Leah says "Everybody gets an 'A' on his or her composition, but only when it meets a high standard, which may take many drafts."
reviews information	Leah "[has] 'writing celebrations' in which students read their finished compositions to the class for applause and comment.

2. KEY CONCEPTS, PRINCIPLES, AND THEORIES

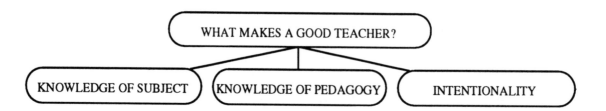

6

II. WHAT IS THE ROLE OF RESEARCH IN EDUCATIONAL PSYCHOLOGY?

1. SELF-CHECK ITEM: In the opening scenario, Leah Washington explains to Ellen Mathis that she uses basic educational psychology to get her students to write. From their discussions, create a list of research-based and common sense teaching strategies that an intentional teacher may use.

- Be purposeful, thoughtful, and flexible, without losing sight of the goals for students.
- Be certain that students are engaged in meaningful activities.
- Ask yourself if the lesson is appropriate to students' background knowledge, skills, and needs.
- Make assignments that meet goals and outcomes.
- Use sound educational research and theories to guide instruction.

2. KEY CONCEPTS, PRINCIPLES, AND THEORIES

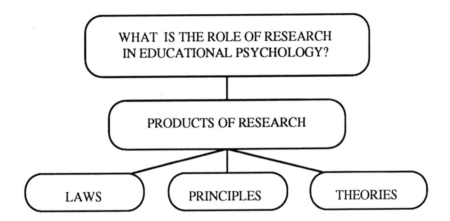

III. WHAT RESEARCH METHODS ARE USED IN EDUCATIONAL PSYCHOLOGY?

1. SELF-CHECK ITEM: Construct a comparison chart with the columns headed Experimental, Correlation, and Descriptive. Enter information in the following five categories: goals of research, forms studies take, kinds of findings, advantages and disadvantages, and examples.

TYPICAL RESPONSE: Construct a comparison chart with the columns headed Experimental, Correlation, and Descriptive. Enter information about goals, forms, findings, advantages and disadvantages, and examples.

TYPE OF RESEARCH: EXPERIMENTAL

GOALS:	test the effectiveness of a treatment
FORMS:	laboratory, randomized-field experiment, single-case study
KINDS OF FINDINGS:	cause and effect
ADVANTAGES AND DISADVANTAGES:	internally valid, little relevance to real-life situations
EXAMPLES:	rewards can diminish interest in an activity (laboratory); a new math teaching strategy was more effective than a traditional method (randomized-field); counting the number of minutes a student is on task using a new reward system (single-case)

TYPE OF RESEARCH: CORRELATIONAL

GOALS: look for relationships between variables
FORMS: positive, negative, unrelated
KINDS OF FINDINGS: shows how variables move together or apart from each other
ADVANTAGES AND DISADVANTAGES: shows relationships, not causes and effects
EXAMPLES: positive relationship between reading and math achievement;
                                      negative relationship between math achievement and days
                                      absent from instruction

TYPE OF RESEARCH: DESCRIPTIVE

GOALS: describe something of interest
FORMS: surveys, interviews, ethnography
KINDS OF FINDINGS: observations of what exists naturally in the environment
ADVANTAGES AND DISADVANTAGES: describes what is, less control over variables
EXAMPLES: describe the consequences of desegregation at a high school

2. KEY CONCEPTS, PRINCIPLES, AND THEORIES

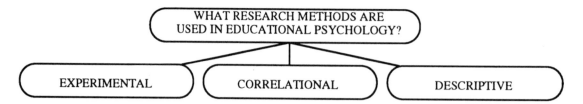

FOR YOUR ENJOYMENT

This section of the study guide includes suggestions for enriching your understanding of a chapter heading you have mastered. You will find information on activities related to the heading and suggestions for research papers, interviews, or presentations.

I. WHAT MAKES A GOOD TEACHER?

1. Make a list of positive personal characteristics that you believe you possess.
   A. For each characteristic, determine if it is essential for good teaching.
   B. Rank order the characteristics from most essential to least essential.
   C. Ask administrators, teachers, and students to rank order your list of characteristics in the same manner as described above. Compare and discuss your lists with others.

2. For a research topic, review the literature on expertise development and its application to teaching.

II. WHAT IS THE ROLE OF RESEARCH IN EDUCATIONAL PSYCHOLOGY?

1. Review some educational psychology and education journals. Make a list of the

type of questions asked by the researchers.

2. Interview teachers about their methods of making educational decisions. Do they use formal or informal research methods?

3. For a research topic, review the literature on teachers as researchers.

III. WHAT RESEARCH METHODS ARE USED IN EDUCATIONAL PSYCHOLOGY?

1. Do teachers call on students with different degrees of frequency? Observe in a classroom for at least one hour. Using a seating chart, keep track of the students who are called on by the teacher. From your data, answer the following questions:
A. If you divide the room into quadrants, does any one quadrant dominate in the number of times students are called on by the teacher? Can you identify any other patterns?
B. If you identify the gender of each student, are males or females called on more often?

2. Identify a question related to educational psychology that you would like to have answered. Design a research study to address your question. Include a statement of the problem as well as the design and procedure you will use to study the question.

3. Review some educational psychology and education journals. What type of research designs are used?

CHAPTER ONE: SELF-ASSESSMENT

DIRECTIONS: Below are questions related to the main ideas presented in the chapter. Correct answers or typical responses can be found at the end of the study guide.

1. Write a paragraph that begins with the following topic sentence: Intentional teachers do things on purpose.

2. Define and provide an example of a principle, a law, and a theory.

3. Match the type of research listed with the advantage it offers.

_____ laboratory experiment	A. has high internal validity and rigorous controls
_____ randomized field experiment	B. involves observation of one individual's behavior over time
_____ single-case experiment	
	C. involves frequent assessments over time

4. Match the following types of experiment with the situations that illustrate each. (A research type may be used more than once or not at all.)

_____ observing and noting how preschoolers play

_____ recording the number of times a student misbehaves, before, during, and after a special reinforcement program

_____ determining the relationship between reading ability and math achievement

_____ evaluating a new teaching technique for a short period of time under highly controlled conditions

A. randomized field experiment

B. descriptive research

C. laboratory experiment

D. correlational study

5. A teacher wants to know if a new teaching strategy is more effective than the traditional one she uses in several tenth grade composition classes. She selects two classes that are the same in ability, then uses the new approach in one class while continuing with the traditional approach in the other class. She then compares compositions written by each group. What type of research is the teacher conducting?

A. experimental
B. correlational
C. descriptive

6. In a hypothetical schoolwide correlational study, the number of days a student was absent during a marking period was shown on the average to have a negative correlation with the student's class ranking from one marking period to the next. This negative correlation would mean that

A. absenteeism causes lower class rankings.
B. the study does not have internal validity.
C. class rankings tend to rise as absenteeism decreases.
D. class rank decreases absenteeism.

7. A type of descriptive research that involves observation in a social setting over an extended period of time is called

A. a randomized field experiment.
B. a correlational study.
C. an ethnographic study.

8. Describe the relationship between subject matter knowledge and pedagogy.

9. Explain why teachers need knowledge of research on teaching as well as common sense.

10. Why do teachers need to study educational psychology?

PRACTICE TEST ANSWERS

1. True; Leadership, humor, and enthusiasm are important personal characteristics of teachers. So are warmth, planning, hard work, self-discipline, a contagious love of learning, speaking ability, and a variety of other characteristics.

2. False; Effective teaching is not a simple matter of one person with more knowledge transmitting that knowledge to another.

3. True; Pedagogy is the link between what the teacher wants students to learn and what students actually learn.

4. B; Intentionality means doing things for a reason, on purpose. Intentional teachers are constantly thinking about the outcomes they want for their students and how each decision they make moves students toward those outcomes.

5. B; Expert teachers are critical thinkers who work to improve their teaching skills.

6. Good teaching has to be observed and practiced, but there are principles of good teaching that can be applied in the classroom, which teachers need to know.

7. Intentional teachers teach with a purpose in mind. They experiment with strategies to solve problems of instruction. They observe the results of their actions to see if they were effective. They constantly ask themselves whether each portion of their lesson was appropriate to students' background knowledge, skills, and needs, whether each activity or assignment was clearly related to a valued outcome, and whether each instructional minute was used wisely and well.

8. True; The goal of research in educational psychology is to examine obvious as well as less obvious questions, using objective methods to test ideas about the factors that contribute to learning.

9. False; The same facts and principles may be interpreted in different ways by different theorists, making progress slow and uneven.

10. C, A, B; Theories are sets of related principles and laws that explain broad aspects of learning. Laws are simply principles that have been thoroughly tested and found to apply to a wide variety of situations. Principles explain relationships between or among factors.

11. C; Many teachers believe that scolding students for misbehavior will improve student behavior. While this is true for many students, for others scolding may be a reward for misbehavior (attention from teacher and peers) and actually increase it.

12. A; Research + Common Sense = Effective Teaching.

13. D; Making the right decision depends on the situation within which the problem arises, the objectives the teacher has in mind, and a combination of research and common sense.

14. Educational research affects educational policies, professional development programs, and teaching materials.

15. C, A, B; Descriptive research includes surveys, interviews, or observations in a social setting. Experimental research creates special treatments and analyzes the effects. Correlational research looks at relationships between variables.

16. A; Laboratory experiments permit researchers to exert a high degree of control over all factors involved in the study, but doing so makes it highly artificial.

17. C; Single-case experiments demonstrate the effects of a treatment on one person or one group by comparing behavior before, during, and after treatment.

18. B; Randomized-field experiments demonstrate the effects of a treatment under realistic conditions.

19. B; A positive correlation shows that as one set of variables increases (reading achievement scores), so does another set (self-esteem scores).

20. C; A negative correlation shows that as one set of variables increases (test scores), the other set decreases (absences).

21. Causal research demonstrates cause and effect relationships while correlational research demonstrates relationships between variables.

2
THEORIES OF DEVELOPMENT

CHAPTER OVERVIEW

The purpose of both this and the next chapter is to discuss major theorists and theories of human development—the ways in which people grow, adapt, and change during their lifetimes. Some of the major theorists' ideas about cognitive, personal/social, and moral development appear below.

Human development is the study of growth, adaptations, and changes that occur in cognition over time. Jean Piaget and Lev Vygotsky studied differences in individuals' thinking and language development.

Human development is the study of growth, adaptations, and changes that occur in personality and social relationships as individuals mature. Erik Erikson devised a lifespan approach to personal/social development.

Human development is the study of growth, adaptations, and changes that occur in moral behavior over time. Jean Piaget, Lawrence Kohlberg, and Martin Hoffman studied how development affects moral reasoning.

CHAPTER OUTLINE

I. WHAT ARE SOME VIEWS OF HUMAN DEVELOPMENT?
    A. Aspects of Development
    B. Issues of Development

II. HOW DID PIAGET VIEW COGNITIVE DEVELOPMENT?
    A. How Development Occurs
    B. Piaget's Stages of Development

III. HOW IS PIAGET'S WORK VIEWED TODAY?
    A. Criticisms and Revisions of Piaget's Theory
    B. Neo-Piagetian, Information Processing and Constructivist Views of Development

IV. HOW DID VYGOTSKY VIEW COGNITIVE DEVELOPMENT?
    A. How Development Occurs
    B. Applications of Vygotskian Theory in Teaching

V. HOW DID ERIKSON VIEW PERSONAL AND SOCIAL DEVELOPMENT?
    A. Stages of Psychosocial Development
    B. Implications and Criticisms of Erikson's Theory

VI. WHAT ARE SOME THEORIES OF MORAL DEVELOPMENT?
    A. Piaget's Theory of Moral Development
    B. Kohlberg's Stages of Moral Reasoning

C. Criticisms of Kohlberg's Theory

D. Hoffman's Development of Moral Behavior

PRACTICE TEST

DIRECTIONS: Each chapter heading from the text listed below is followed by a series of related questions worth a total of ten points. Respond to each question, check your answers with those found at the end of the study guide chapter, then determine your score. Consider nine points per heading to be mastery.

For those headings on which you do not score at least nine points, turn to the FOR YOUR INFORMATION section of the study guide for corrective instruction. For those headings on which you do score at least nine points, turn to the FOR YOUR ENJOYMENT section of the study guide for enrichment activities.

I. WHAT ARE SOME VIEWS OF HUMAN DEVELOPMENT?

True or False

1. (1 point) _____ Development refers to the changes in physical, personal, social, cognitive, and moral characteristics that occur over one's lifespan.

2. (1 point) _____ Children are like miniature adults; their thinking is qualitatively the same as adults' thinking.

3. (1 point) _____ One of the first requirements of effective teaching is that the teacher understand how students think and view the world.

4. (3 points)

Matching

_____ major developmental theorist who studied cognition   A. Erikson

B. Kohlberg

_____ major developmental theorist who studied moral reasoning   C. Piaget

_____ major developmental theorist who studied personal growth and social relationships

Short Answer/Essay

5. (2 points)   Describe the nature vs. nurture controversy.

_____

_____

6. (2 points)   Define and give an example of a discontinuous theory of development. Define and give an example of a continuous theory of development.

_____

_____

II. HOW DID PIAGET VIEW COGNITIVE DEVELOPMENT?

Sentence Completion

7. (1 point) _____ are mental patterns that guide thinking and behavior.

8. (1 point) _____ is the process of incorporating new information into existing schemes.

9. (1 point) _____ is the process of modifying existing schemes so that new knowledge can be understood.

10. (4 points)

Matching

_____ Inferred reality—the ability to see things in context—is a characteristic of an individual who is at this stage.

    A. sensorimotor

_____ Hypothetical thought—the ability to deal with possibilities—is a characteristic of an individual who is at this stage.

    B. preoperations

    C. concrete operations

    D. formal operations

_____ Object permanence—knowing that an object exists when it is out of sight—is a characteristic of an individual who is at the end of this stage.

_____ Egocentric behavior—believing that everyone shares his or her beliefs—is a characteristic of an individual who is at this stage.

Multiple Choice

11. (1 point) _____ Which of the following is an example of conservation?

A. A student is able to explain why the amount of water poured from a short, wide beaker into a tall, narrow beaker remains constant.
B. A student can select one choice from a variety of alternatives in order to form a hypothesis.
C. A student who used to call all small animals "kitty" can now discriminate between a cat and a skunk.
D. A student can place 10 sticks of various lengths in order from shortest to tallest.

12. (1 point) _____ At the end of Piaget's concrete operational stage, a child is capable of all of the following tasks except

A. class inclusion.
B. transitivity.
C. decentration.
D. testing hypotheses.

15

13. (1 point) _____ The abilities that make up formal operational thought are critical to learning which of the following cognitive tasks?

    A. conservation
    B. higher-order thinking skills
    C. assimilation and accommodation
    D. equilibration

III. HOW IS PIAGET'S WORK VIEWED TODAY?

True or False

14. (1 point) _____ Piaget believed that developmental stages are fixed—that certain cognitive tasks cannot be completed until the individual is developmentally ready.

15. (1 point) _____ Recent research demonstrates that children are more competent than Piaget originally thought.

16. (1 point) _____ Neo-Piagetians have found that Piaget's beliefs about children's egocentrism—seeing only their own point of view—remains accurate even when familiar tasks and age-appropriate language are used in testing.

Multiple Choice

17. (1 point) _____ Information processing theorists disagree with Piaget on which of the following points?

    A. the description of cognition
    B. development precedes learning
    C. thinking skills can be directly taught
    D. learning is culture- and context-free

18. (1 point) _____ Neo-Piagetians have demonstrated that learners' abilities to operate at a particular stage depend on all of the following circumstances except

    A. the specific task involved.
    B. the training received.
    C. experience.
    D. exposure to computers.

19. (1 point) _____ Which of the following approaches represents an information processing view of development?

    A. rule-assessment
    B. stage theory
    C. self-regulation
    D. scaffolding

Short Answer/Essay

20. (4 points) List four criticisms of Piaget's work.

_____

_____

_____

_____

IV. HOW DID VYGOTSKY VIEW COGNITIVE DEVELOPMENT?

True or False

21. (1 point) _____ One important contribution of Vygotsky's theory is that it emphasizes the sociocultural nature of learning.

22. (1 point) _____ According to Vygotsky, mental functioning exists within the individual before it exists in conservation and collaboration.

Sentence Completion

23. (1 point) _____ is a term used to describe a developmental phase of learning in which a learner will fail at a task if attempted independently, but not if she or he is given support.

24. (1 point) _____ is a mechanism for turning shared knowledge into personal knowledge.

25. (1 point) _____ involves providing a learner with support during the early stages of learning and then encouraging him or her to take on greater responsibility as the task becomes more familiar.

26. (1 point) _____ is a teaching approach that emphasizes scaffolding and private speech to solve problems.

Short Answer/Essay

27. (4 points) List two major educational implications of Vygotsky's theory and give an example of each.

_____

_____

_____

_____

V. HOW DID ERIKSON VIEW PERSONAL AND SOCIAL DEVELOPMENT?

True or False

28. (1 point) _____ Erikson proposed that individuals pass through eight psychosocial stages with a crisis to be resolved at each stage.

29. (1 point) _____ Most people resolve developmental crises as they pass through the psychosocial stages, but some do not. Thus, they end up dealing with them later in life.

30. (1 point) _____ Erikson's theory de-emphasizes the role of the environment, both in causing a crisis and in determining how it will be resolved.

31 (4 points)   *Matching*

_____ stage where "Who am I?" becomes important

_____ stage where the focus is "I am what I learn"

_____ stage of exploration of the physical and social environment

_____ stage dedicated to finding oneself in another

A. initiative vs. guilt

B. industry vs. inferiority

C. identity vs. role confusion

D. intimacy vs. isolation

Short Answer/Essay

32. (3 points) List an educational experience that will help develop:
1) initiative; 2) industry; and 3) identity.

_____

_____

VI. WHAT ARE SOME THEORIES OF MORAL DEVELOPMENT?

Sentence Completion

33. (1 point) _____ is a type of moral reasoning in which an individual believes that rules are fixed and unchangeable, according to Piaget.

34. (1 point) _____ is a type of moral reasoning in which an individual considers a transgressor's intentions, according to Piaget.

35. (1 point) _____ is a structured moral situation, developed by Kohlberg.

36. (3 points)   *Matching*

_____ level of moral reasoning in which individuals obey authority figures to avoid punishment

_____ level of moral reasoning in which individuals use ethical principles to guide moral behavior

_____ level of moral reasoning in which individuals follow social rules

A. preconventional

B. conventional

C. postconventional

Multiple Choice

37. (1 point) _____ Individuals progress from stage to stage by

A. interacting with those whose moral reasoning is at a higher level.
B. resolving critical and conflicting psychosocial issues.
C. exhibiting socially acceptable behavior.
D. seeking approval and avoiding punishment.

38. (1 point) _____ Martin Hoffman's theory of moral development compliments the work of Piaget and Kohlberg by acknowledging

    A. other experts in the field.
    B. the role of cognition in explaining moral behavior.
    C. that guilt plays no role in moral behavior.
    D. that students should essentially be left to develop on their own.

Short Answer/Essay

39. (2 points) List two limitations of Kohlberg's theory of moral development.

_____

_____

SCORING	POINTS NEEDED FOR MASTERY	POINTS RECEIVED
I. WHAT ARE SOME VIEWS OF HUMAN DEVELOPMENT?	9	
II. HOW DID PIAGET VIEW HUMAN DEVELOPMENT?	9	
III. HOW IS PIAGET'S WORK VIEWED TODAY?	9	
IV. HOW DID VYGOTSKY VIEW COGNITIVE DEVELOPMENT?	9	
V. HOW DID ERIKSON VIEW PERSONAL AND SOCIAL DEVELOPMENT?	9	
VI. WHAT ARE SOME THEORIES OF MORAL DEVELOPMENT?	9	

FOR YOUR INFORMATION

This section of the study guide includes suggestions for further study of the information you have not yet mastered. You will find information on: 1) typical responses to the SELF-CHECK item(s) from the text; and 2) key concepts, principles, and theories addressed in the text chapter.

I. WHAT ARE SOME VIEWS OF HUMAN DEVELOPMENT?

1. SELF-CHECK ITEM: Begin a four-column comparison chart with the columns headed Piaget, Vygotsky, Erikson, and Kohlberg. Identify the theory that each proposed, the type of development involved, and whether the theory is continuous or discontinuous. After you finish reading the chapter, explain the three chapter-opening scenarios in terms of the theories and concepts presented in the chapter.

TYPICAL RESPONSE: Begin a comparison chart of Piaget, Vygotsky, Erikson, and Kohlberg.

PIAGET	VYGOTSKY	ERIKSON	KOHLBERG
development depends on manipulation and active interaction with the environment	development depends on the sociocultural nature of learning	development depends on the resolution of psychosocial crises	development depends on reasoning about rules that govern behavior
cognitive (discontinuous)	cognitive (discontinuous)	personal/social (discontinuous)	moral (discontinuous)

TYPICAL RESPONSE: Explain the opening vignettes in terms of theories and concepts presented.

Mr. Jones: The teacher's students are preoperational (Piaget's second stage of cognitive development). This means that the children cannot reverse operations, focus on more than one aspect of a problem at a time, or consider another point of view.

Ms. Quintera: Ms. Quintera's student, Frank, is working on resolving issues of identity (Erikson's fourth stage of psychosocial development), which involve breaking away from parents and from those who exhibit "parental" behaviors—teachers.

Ms. Lewis: Ms. Lewis' students are in Piaget's stage of heteronomous morality or Kohlberg's preconventional level of moral development where rules are absolute and punishment is consistent, regardless of intent.

2. KEY CONCEPTS, PRINCIPLES, AND THEORIES

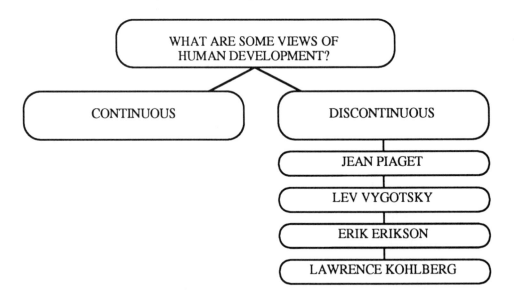

II. HOW DID PIAGET VIEW COGNITIVE DEVELOPMENT?

1. SELF-CHECK ITEM: Think of an original example from your own experience or observation for each of the following phenomena, as described by Piaget: scheme,

assimilation, accommodation, equilibration. Add Piaget's four stages of development to the comparison chart you started in the first Self-Check. Then, classify the following capabilities in terms of Piaget's stages: inferred reality, reflexes, abstract thinking, object permanence, egocentrism, use of symbols, centration, use of logic, reversibility, goal direction, conservation, perceived appearances, reciprocity, inversion, and class inclusion. At what stage is each one achieved? Give an example of each.

TYPICAL RESPONSE: Think of an original example of scheme, assimilation, accommodation, and equilibration.

Piagetian Term	Example
scheme	Organizing your understanding of trees into coniferous and deciduous.
assimilation	A child I know believed the earth is flat because the horizon is flat. When told that the earth is round, she thought: round and flat, like a disk.
accommodation	My niece just learned that hymns are not "boys' songs" (hims).
equilibration	Trying to remember someone's name when I can't (disequilibration), then suddenly remembering it (equilibration).

TYPICAL RESPONSE: Add Piaget's stages of development and tasks to be accomplished at each stage to your chart.

PIAGET

STAGE	TASKS	EXAMPLES
sensorimotor	object permanence	looking for a toy when it is out of sight
	reflexes	placing your finger in the palm of an infant's hand and the infant grasping it
	use of symbols	using words to represent thought ("Mama")
	goal direction	pulling on a blanket holding a toy that is out of reach
preoperational	centration	considering height, but not width, when solving a problem that involves both
	perceived appearances	thinking the sun sets (goes down below the earth)
	egocentrism	thinking that farmers have cows so you can look at them
concrete operational	inferred reality	knowing the illusion of the sun setting is caused by the rotation of the earth
	reversibility	knowing that 7 + 5 = 12 can be reversed to show that 12 - 5 = 7
	inversion	knowing that 1/2 is different from 2/1
	classification	arranging dinosaurs into meat eaters and plant eaters
	conservation	knowing that the volume of a liquid poured from one container to another remains constant
formal	use of logic	reasoning through an analytic problem
	abstract thinking	thinking what it would have been like had Germany won World War II

2. KEY CONCEPTS, PRINCIPLES, AND THEORIES

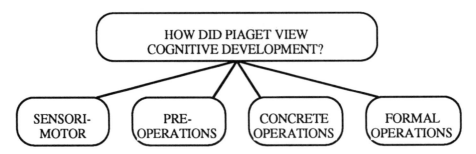

III. HOW IS PIAGET'S WORK VIEWED TODAY?

1. SELF-CHECK ITEM: List four general teaching implications of Piagetian principles. Describe a teaching strategy that applies Piagetian concepts in the classroom. Summarize the arguments against Piaget's theory of cognitive development.

TYPICAL RESPONSE: List four general Piagetian principles.

> Focus on the process of students' thinking, not just the products.
> Recognize the crucial role of the learner's self-initiated, active involvement in learning activities.
> De-emphasize practices aimed at making children adult-like in their thinking.
> Accept individual differences in developmental progress.

TYPICAL RESPONSE: Describe a teaching strategy that applies Piagetian concepts in the classroom.

> Classroom Strategy: Discovery
> Present a puzzling situation well matched to the learner's developmental stage.
> Elicit student responses and ask for justification. Offer counter-suggestions and probe for responses.
> Present related tasks and probe students' reasoning. Offer counter-suggestions to see if learned ideas transfer to new, but related ideas.

TYPICAL RESPONSE: Summarize the arguments against Piaget's theory of cognitive development.

argument: Piaget underestimated children's cognitive ability. Researchers have found that children can complete some cognitive tasks that are beyond their stage of reasoning if the task and language are familiar. Piaget counter-argues that these children are "developmentally ready" and that is why they can accomplish the tasks.

argument: Piaget's notion of egocentrism occurs to a lesser degree than he described. Researchers have found that children can consider another's point of view if it is practical and familiar in context.

argument: Piaget's notion of stages is not as clear as he thought. Some children can be in a higher stage for familiar tasks and a lower stage for less familiar tasks.

2. KEY CONCEPTS, PRINCIPLES, AND THEORIES

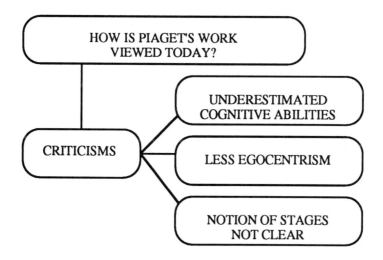

IV. HOW DID VYGOTSKY VIEW COGNITIVE DEVELOPMENT?

1. SELF-CHECK ITEM: On your comparison chart of theorists, enter information comparing the views of Piaget and Vygotsky on the nature of learning and the context in which learning takes place. Describe a teaching strategy that applies Vygotskian concepts in the classroom.

TYPICAL RESPONSE: On your chart, compare the views of Piaget and Vygotsky.

	PIAGET	VYGOTSKY
NATURE OF LEARNING	learning occurs as an individual seeks equilibration	learning occurs when students are within their zone of proximal development
CONTEXT	assimilation and accommodation	turn shared knowledge into personal knowledge

TYPICAL RESPONSE: Describe a teaching strategy that applies Vygotskian principles in the classroom.

strategy: Provide learners with support during the early stages of learning, then diminish support and have them take on increasing responsibility as they are able (scaffolding).

strategy: Test both levels of the zone of proximal development to determine learners' current states (dynamic assessment).

2. KEY CONCEPTS, PRINCIPLES, AND THEORIES

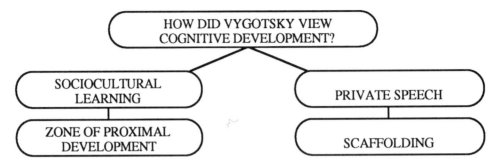

V. HOW DID ERIKSON VIEW PERSONAL AND SOCIAL DEVELOPMENT?

1. SELF-CHECK ITEM: Compare Erikson's eight stages of psychosocial development to Piaget's four stages of cognitive development on your comparison chart. Which of Erikson's stages pertain to preschool, elementary school, middle school, and secondary school students? Think of an example in which an individual experiences and then successfully resolves each psychosocial crisis that occurs before and during the school years. In each instance, give an example of how a parent or teacher might help an individual to resolve the development crisis in a positive way.

TYPICAL RESPONSE: Compare Piaget with Erikson and show how each pertains to students.

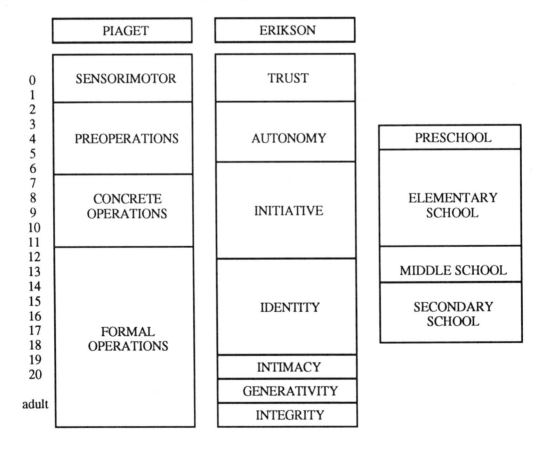

24

TYPICAL RESPONSE: Give an example of how a parent or teacher might help individuals to successfully resolve tasks.

STAGES	EXAMPLE	POSITIVE RESOLUTION
initiative vs. guilt	learning language	whole language approach where children explore structure and meaning of words
industry vs. inferiority	learning to relate to others outside the family	provide opportunities for children to interact with peers
identity vs. role confusion	answer question "Who am I?"	provide adolescents with opportunities to "try on" roles

2. KEY CONCEPTS, PRINCIPLES, AND THEORIES

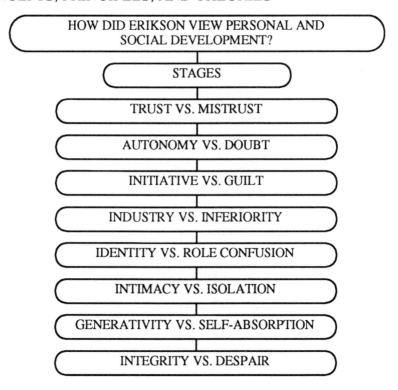

HOW DID ERIKSON VIEW PERSONAL AND SOCIAL DEVELOPMENT?

STAGES

TRUST VS. MISTRUST

AUTONOMY VS. DOUBT

INITIATIVE VS. GUILT

INDUSTRY VS. INFERIORITY

IDENTITY VS. ROLE CONFUSION

INTIMACY VS. ISOLATION

GENERATIVITY VS. SELF-ABSORPTION

INTEGRITY VS. DESPAIR

VI. WHAT ARE SOME THEORIES OF MORAL DEVELOPMENT?

1. SELF-CHECK ITEM: On your comparison chart, compare Piaget's two stages of moral development to Kohlberg's six stages of moral reasoning. By what ages do individuals seem capable of each level of thinking? Think of an original example of a moral dilemma and show how different individuals' judgements would illustrate each of Kohlberg's levels.

TYPICAL RESPONSE: Compare Piaget's two stages of moral development to Kohlberg's six stages on your comparison chart. By what school levels do students seem capable of each level of thinking?

25

PIAGET		KOHLBERG
elementary	heteronomous morality (under six) autonomous morality (over six)	level one: preconventional (under 10)
secondary		level two: conventional (10-20) level three: postconventional (over 20)

TYPICAL RESPONSE: Think of an original example of a moral dilemma and show how different individuals' judgements would illustrate each of Kohlberg's levels. In each case, how might a parent or teacher help a learner to grow?

example: Jake is an average math student and so are his two friends, Margaret and Bill. Before an upcoming weekly exam, Margaret and Bill steal a test copy from the teacher's desk. They ask Jake if he would like to look at the copy, but he declines. Jake decides to tell the teacher about Margaret and Bill stealing the test.

Level One: Jake tells the teacher because he is afraid of being implicated in the theft. He does not want to be punished. He may even be rewarded by the teacher for his act of honesty.

Level Two: Jake wants to please his teacher. Also, rules are rules—no cheating.

Level Three: Jake, being a person of principle, could not disregard the agreement of the class to not cheat or his own belief that cheating is ethically wrong.

Kohlberg believed that individuals progress from one stage to the next by interacting with others whose reasoning is one or two stages above their own. Parents and teachers then need to identify the stage at which an individual is reasoning, and then present examples of higher levels of reasoning about the same issue for her or him to consider.

2. KEY CONCEPTS, PRINCIPLES, AND THEORIES

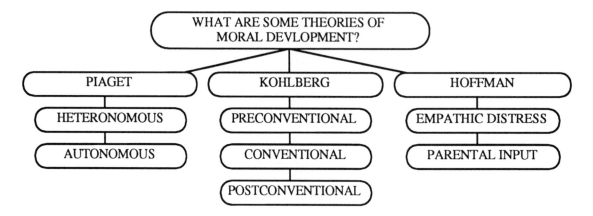

FOR YOUR ENJOYMENT

This section of the study guide includes suggestions for enriching your understanding of a chapter heading you have mastered. You will find information on activities related to the headings and suggestions for research papers, interviews, or presentations.

I. WHAT ARE SOME VIEWS OF HUMAN DEVELOPMENT?

1. Discuss the following controversies about development.
   A. Is development continuous or discontinuous?
   B. Is development universal or do culture, gender, or socioeconomic status play a role?

2. For a research topic, review the literature on cognitive, psychosocial, or moral development. What trends have emerged since Piaget, Erikson, or Kohlberg developed their theories?

II. HOW DID PIAGET VIEW COGNITIVE DEVELOPMENT?

1. Ask children the following questions, then discuss the implications of the responses you receive.
   A. Where does the sun come from in the morning? Where does the sun go at night?
   B. Where do dreams come from? Where do they go when you wake up?
   C. When is yesterday? When is tomorrow?

2. Design a lesson plan for concrete operational children or formal operational adolescents that addresses the important cognitive tasks of the stage.

3. Critique a teacher's manual. Does it address important Piagetian concepts? Are the lesson suggestions developmentally appropriate?

4. For a research topic, review the literature on Piaget and his contributions to education.

III. HOW IS PIAGET'S WORK VIEWED TODAY?

1. Ask children of different ages (e.g., ages 4, 7, and 11) to solve conservation problems as posed by Piaget. Adapt the problems so that their context and language are familiar to the child. Are there differences in the how the child solves unfamiliar and familiar tasks?

2. For a research topic, review the literature on neo-Piagetian, information processing, and constructivists views of cognitive development.

IV. HOW DID VYGOTSKY VIEW COGNITIVE DEVELOPMENT?

1. For a research topic, review the related literature on Vygotsky and his contributions to education.

V. HOW DID ERIKSON VIEW PERSONAL AND SOCIAL DEVELOPMENT?

1. Design a lesson that addresses the psychosocial needs of students who are at the age you intend to teach.

2. For a research topic, review the related literature on Erikson and his contributions to education.

VI. WHAT ARE SOME THEORIES OF MORAL DEVELOPMENT?

1. Interview five people using Kohlberg's "Heinz" dilemma. Analyze the responses.

2. For a research topic, review the related literature on Kohlberg and his contributions to education.

CHAPTER TWO: SELF-ASSESSMENT

DIRECTIONS: Below are questions related to the main ideas presented in the chapter. Correct answers or typical responses can be found at the end of the study guide.

1. Which of the following pairs of issues are central in developmental psychology?

      A. assimilation and accommodation
      B. nature versus nurture and continuous versus discontinuous development
      C. preconventional thinking and postconventional thinking
      D. zone of proximal development versus private speech and scaffolding

2. Match each of the following stages of cognitive development with its definition.

_____ sensorimotor	A. Exploration of the environment occurs mostly through the use of the five senses and motor skills.
_____ preoperational	
_____ concrete operational	B. Learners are capable of hypothetical, abstract thought and scientific reasoning
_____ formal operational	C. Learners make errors when attempting to solve conservation tasks because they center on one aspect of the problem.
	D. Inferable reality, seriation, and transitivity are cognitive skills possessed by these learners.

3. Write a brief paragraph explaining the difference between assimilation and accommodation.

4. Piaget's principles have been criticized because recent research demonstrates that

      A. many children go through cognitive stages in varying orders.
      B. cognitive tasks such as conservation cannot be taught unless the child is in the appropriate stage.
      C. the clarity of task instruction can significantly influence young children's performance on conservation tasks.
      D. children, on the average, are actually less competent than Piaget thought.

5. Vygotsky suggested that when students are capable of learning but have not yet learned, teachers should assist them by using any of the following methods except

    A. social interaction and private speech.
    B. assisted discovery and problem solving.
    C. perceived appearances.
    D. scaffolding.

6. A typical individual who is in Piaget's stage of concrete operations is, at the same time, in Erikson's stage of

    A. autonomy versus doubt.
    B. industry versus inferiority.
    C. intimacy versus isolation.
    D. generativity versus self-absorption.

7. The psychosocial stage associated with adolescence is

    A. identity versus role confusion.
    B. industry versus inferiority.
    C. intimacy versus isolation.
    D. integrity versus despair.

8. Match each level of Kohlberg's theory of moral development with its definition.

_____ preconventional

_____ conventional

_____ postconventional

A. Self-chosen, ethical principles guide moral decision making.

B. The self is of the greatest concern.

C. Moral decisions are made to satisfy the needs of the group and to maintain the social order.

9. Describe Hoffman's theory of moral behavior and parenting. What is empathic distress?

10. Describe typical preoperational, concrete operational, and formal operational learners (i.e., they are developing as the theorists proposed); then, add statements about their psychosocial and moral development.

PRACTICE TEST ANSWERS

1. True; Development refers to the relatively permanent changes that occur over a lifespan.

2. False; Children are not miniature adults. Their thinking is quantitatively and qualitatively different from adult thinking.

3. True; Effective teachers take into account students' ages and stages of development.

4. C, B, A; Piaget studied cognition, Erikson studied personal growth and social relationships, and Kohlberg studied moral development (as did Piaget; however, Kohlberg is considered the major theorist).

5. Some individuals believe that development is predetermined at birth, by heredity and biological factors (nature), while others believe that development is determined by environmental factors (nurture). Most development psychologists believe that nature and nurture combine to influence development.

6. Discontinuous theories address development as a series of stages with major tasks to be accomplished at each stage. Piaget, Erikson, and Kohlberg are all discontinuous developmental theorists. Continuous theories address development as a smooth progression from infancy to adulthood. An example of a continuous developmental theory would be information processing.

7. Schemes; Schemes are mental patterns or building blocks used to organize thinking.

8. Assimilation; Assimilation is the process of incorporating new objects or events into existing schemes.

9. Accommodation; Accommodation is the process of changing an existing scheme so that new objects or events can be understood.

10. C, D, A, B; Inferred reality occurs at the concrete operational stage, hypothetical thought is a product of formal operations, object permanence is a sensorimotor stage task, and egocentric behavior occurs during preoperations, according to Piaget.

11. A; Conservation is the ability to understand that even though a variable changes in appearance (as when water is poured from a short, wide beaker into a tall, narrow one), other characteristics (volume) remain constant.

12. D; Hypothesis testing is a characteristic of formal operations.

13. B; The abilities that make up formal operational thought—thinking abstractly, testing hypotheses, and forming concepts independent of physical reality—are critical in the learning of higher order thinking skills.

14. True; Piaget held the belief that development precedes learning, that developmental stages are largely fixed, and that certain cognitive tasks require readiness.

15. True; Researchers today have found that children are more competent than Piaget originally thought, especially when their practical knowledge is assessed.

16. False; Researchers have found that children can consider another's point of view if the context is practical and familiar.

17. C; Information processing theorists tend to agree with Piaget's description of cognition; but, unlike Piaget, they believe that thinking skills can be directly taught.

18. D; Neo-Piagetians have demonstrated that an individual's ability to operate at a particular stage depends a great deal on the specific task involved and that training and experience, including social interactions, can accelerate development.

19. A; Learners acquire increasingly powerful rules or procedures for solving problems and can be stimulated to discover deficiencies in their logic and to apply new logical principles.

20. Criticisms of Piaget's work include: 1) there may be more than four stages of cognitive development; 2) development of stages is somewhat flexible, not fixed; 3) in practical contexts, preoperational children can consider the views of others; and 4) children are competent learners.

21. True; Vygotsky emphasized the sociocultural nature of learning.

22. False; Vygotsky believed mental functioning exists within conversation and collaboration before it exists within the individual.

23. Zone of Proximal Development; The term refers to a phase of learning in which the learner will fail alone, but succeed with assistance.

24. Private Speech; A mechanism emphasized by Vygotsky for turning shared speech into personal knowledge is private speech.

25. Scaffolding; Scaffolding means providing a learner with support during the early stages of learning and then diminishing that support.

26. Assisted Discovery; This is a scaffolding approach in which teachers explicitly help students use private speech to talk themselves through problems.

27. One implication of Vygotsky's theory is to expose learners to effective problem solving strategies that fall within their zones. An example of this is cooperative learning. A second implication is to incorporate scaffolding into lessons. Reciprocal teaching and assisted discovery are examples that use scaffolding.

28. True; Erikson proposed that individuals pass through eight stages with tasks at each stage.

29. True; When crises are not resolved, they reoccur later.

30. False; Erikson believed the opposite—that the environment played a major role in causing and resolving developmental crises.

31. C, B, A, D; Attending to the question "Who am I?" develops identity. Focusing on "I am what I learn" develops industry. Exploring the physical and social environment develops initiative. Finding oneself in another develops intimacy.

32. Initiative can be developed through exploration of the environment. Industry can be developed by allowing children to try things independently. Identity can be developed by supporting adolescents as they "try on" different adult roles.

33. Heteronomous Morality; This is a type of moral reasoning in which rules are fixed and made by others.

34. Autonomous Morality; This type of moral reasoning incorporates intentions and circumstances into the decision.

35. Moral Dilemma; Kohlberg's structured moral situations are called dilemmas.

36. A, C, B; At the preconventional level, individuals obey rules to avoid punishment. At the conventional level, individuals follow social rules. At the postconventional level, individuals use self-determined ethical principles to guide behavior.

37. A; According to Kohlberg, individuals move to higher levels of moral reasoning as they are exposed to them through others.

38. B; Hoffman's theory of moral development compliments Piaget and Kohlberg because it recognizes the role of cognitive abilities and reasoning skills in explaining moral behavior.

39. Limitations of Kohlberg's theory include: 1) Kohlberg's research was conducted using males, then generalized to females; and 2) Kohlberg's theory deals with moral reasoning rather than moral behavior.

3
DEVELOPMENT DURING CHILDHOOD AND ADOLESCENCE

CHAPTER OVERVIEW

The purpose of this chapter is to expand upon the information presented in the previous chapter by addressing changes in physical, cognitive, and socioemotional development during the early childhood, elementary, middle, and high school years. Each period of development is described briefly below.

Development during the early childhood years involves the strengthening of large and small motor movements, the acquisition of language, the transition from sensorimotor to preoperational thought, and the formation of initiative.

Development during the elementary years involves tremendous physical growth, the transition from preoperational to concrete operational thought, a movement away from parent and family relations and toward peers, and the formation of industry.

Development during the middle and high school years involves puberty, the transition from concrete operational to formal operational thought, a dependence on peer relationships, and the formation of identity.

CHAPTER OUTLINE

I. HOW DO CHILDREN DEVELOP DURING THE PRESCHOOL YEARS?
   A. Physical Development in Early Childhood
   B. Language Acquisition
   C. Bilingual Education
   D. Socioemotional Development

II. WHAT KINDS OF EARLY CHILDHOOD EDUCATION EXIST?
   A. Day Care Programs
   B. Nursery Schools
   C. Compensatory Preschool Programs
   D. Early Intervention
   E. Kindergarten Programs
   F. Developmentally Appropriate Practice

III. HOW DO CHILDREN DEVELOP DURING THE ELEMENTARY YEARS?
   A. Physical Development During Middle Childhood
   B. Cognitive Abilities
   C. Socioemotional Development in Middle Childhood

IV. HOW DO CHILDREN DEVELOP DURING THE MIDDLE AND HIGH SCHOOL YEARS?
- A. Physical Development During Adolescence
- B. Cognitive Development
- C. Characteristics of Hypothetical-Deductive Reasoning
- D. Implications for Educational Practice
- E. Socioemotional Development During Adolescence
- F. Identity Development
- G. Marcia's Four Identity Statuses
- H. Self-Concept and Self-Esteem
- I. Social Relationships
- J. Emotional Development
- K. Problems of Adolescence

PRACTICE TEST

DIRECTIONS: Each chapter heading from the text listed below is followed by a series of related questions worth a total of ten points. Respond to each question, check your answers with those found at the end of the chapter, then determine your score. Consider nine points per heading to be mastery.

For those headings on which you do not score at least nine points, turn to the FOR YOUR INFORMATION section of the study guide for corrective instruction. For those headings on which you do score at least nine points, turn to the FOR YOUR ENJOYMENT section of the study guide for enrichment activities.

I. HOW DO CHILDREN DEVELOP DURING THE PRESCHOOL YEARS?

True or False

1. (1 point) _____ A major physical accomplishment for children during the preschool years is an increase in control over large (gross) muscle activity and, to a lesser extent, over small (fine) muscle activity.

2. (1 point) _____ During the preschool years, children develop verbal (spoken) language, independent reading skills, and the fundamentals of writing.

Sentence Completion

3. (1 point) _____ is a term used to describe preschool children's understanding of print—that letters represent sounds, that spaces between words have meaning, and that books have a front and a back.

4. (1 point) _____ is the term used to describe a range of teaching practices that emphasizes students reading entire stories, articles, and other real materials rather than concentrating on isolated reading skills.

5. (1 point)   _____   *Multiple Choice*
According to Erikson, preschool children are attempting to resolve which of the following socioemotional issues?

A. initiative vs. guilt
B. trust vs. mistrust
C. identity vs. role confusion
D. intimacy vs. isolation

6. (1 point)   _____   In the year 2020, which of the following numbers represents the number of U.S. children who will not speak English as their primary language?

A. 1 million
B. 10 million
C. 50 million
D. 75 million

7. (1 point)   _____   All of the following are types of collaborative efforts that promote healthy partnerships between parents and schools except

A. involvement in decision making, governance, and advocacy.
B. teachers who provide at-home services.
C. involvement with community organizations.
D. parent volunteers who assist teachers in the classroom.

8. (3 points)   *Short Answer/Essay*
Briefly describe how friendships, prosocial behaviors, and play contribute to healthy socioemotional development.

_____
_____
_____
_____
_____

II. WHAT KINDS OF EARLY CHILDHOOD EDUCATION PROGRAMS EXIST?

9. (1 point)   _____   *True or False*
Almost all countries of the world recognize that the beginning of formal school occurs when children are about six years old.

10. (1 point)   _____   There is widespread agreement regarding schooling practices for children who are under six years of age.

11. (5 points) *Matching*

_____ programs that exist primarily to provide child-care services for working parents

_____ planned programs where children learn "readiness" skills that prepare them for formal instruction

_____ programs such as Head Start for children from disadvantaged backgrounds

_____ programs that facilitate development for infants (from six months) and young children from disadvantaged backgrounds

_____ programs just prior to first grade that prepare students for formal instruction by encouraging social skill development

A. compensatory preschool

B. day care

C. early intervention

D. kindergarten

E. nursery school

12. (3 points) *Short Answer/Essay*

List three characteristics associated with developmentally appropriate educational practices.

_____

_____

_____

III. HOW DO CHILDREN DEVELOP DURING THE ELEMENTARY YEARS?

13. (1 point) _____ *True or False*

During the elementary years, physical development speeds up in comparison with earlier childhood.

14. (1 point) _____ "Transescents" are those individuals who are moving from early to middle childhood.

15. (1 point) _____ Between the ages of five and seven, children make the transition from preoperations to concrete operations.

16. (1 point) _____ *Multiple Choice*

An important area of personal and social development for elementary children is

A. identity.
B. generativity.
C. self-concept.
D. morality.

17. (1 point) _____ Which of the following statements can be attributed to preadolescent development?

A. Major growth spurts for preadolescents begin at about fourth grade for boys and at about sixth grade for girls.
B. While preadolescents feel their parents love them, they do not think they are understood.
C. Preadolescents are beginning the transition from preoperational to concrete operational thought.
D. A major concern of preadolescents is the development of initiative.

Short Answer/Essay

18. (2 points) List three approaches that parents tend to use in disciplining their children.

_____
_____
_____

19. (3 points) List three emotional concerns related to the physical, cognitive, and social development of adolescents.

_____
_____
_____

IV. HOW DO CHILDREN DEVELOP DURING THE MIDDLE AND HIGH SCHOOL YEARS?

True or False

20. (1 point) _____ Early adolescence is a time of rapid physical and intellectual development. Middle adolescence is a time of adjustment to these changes. Later adolescence is a time of transition from childhood to adulthood.

21. (1 point) _____ Puberty is a series of physiological changes that renders the immature organism capable of reproduction.

22. (1 point) _____ Researchers believe that those who enter puberty early have an easier time adjusting to the physiological changes than those who enter puberty later in adolescence.

Multiple Choice

23. (1 point) _____ According to Piaget, adolescence is a time of transition from

A. identity vs. role confusion to intimacy vs. isolation.
B. preoperations to concrete operations.
C. initiative vs. guilt to identity vs. role confusion.
D. concrete operations to formal operations.

24. (1 point) _____ All of the following class activities are designed to promote hypothetical-deductive thought except

A. have students write a paper that requires them to look at more than one side of an issue.
B. have students memorize definitions of terms.
C. have students participate in a mock debate.
D. have students critique their own position papers on a controversial topic.

25. (1 point) _____ Which of the following terms means "a tendency to think about what is going on in one's own mind"?

A. reflectivity
B. cognition
C. hypothetical thought
D. inductive thought

26. (1 point) _____ Which of the following is a term used by Erikson to describe "not having a sense of one's identity"?

A. conformity
B. identity diffusion
C. autonomy
D. identity foreclosure

Short Answer/Essay
27. (3 points) List three problems associated with adolescence.

_____
_____
_____

SCORING	POINTS NEEDED FOR MASTERY	POINTS RECEIVED
I. HOW DO CHILDREN DEVELOP DURING THE PRESCHOOL YEARS?	9	
II. WHAT KINDS OF EARLY CHILDHOOD EDUCATION PROGRAMS EXIST?	9	
III. HOW DO CHILDREN DEVELOP DURING THE ELEMENTARY YEARS?	9	
IV. HOW DO CHILDREN DEVELOP DURING THE MIDDLE AND HIGH SCHOOL YEARS?	9	

FOR YOUR INFORMATION

This section of the study guide includes suggestions for further study of the information you have not yet mastered. You will find information on: 1) typical responses to the SELF-CHECK item(s) from the text; and 2) key concepts, principles, and theories addressed in the text chapter.

I. HOW DO CHILDREN DEVELOP DURING THE PRESCHOOL YEARS?

1. SELF-CHECK ITEM: Begin a comparison chart with the columns headed Early Childhood, Middle Childhood, and Adolescence. Enter information concerning early childhood using the following categories: relevant ages, relevant grade level, Piagetian stages, Eriksonian stages, characteristics of behavior, examples of social relationships, physical characteristics, examples of physical attributes, characteristics of language and thought, and sources of impact on development.

TYPICAL RESPONSE: Begin a comparison chart on early childhood.

	EARLY CHILDHOOD	MIDDLE CHILDHOOD	ADOLESCENCE
AGES	three to five		
GRADE LEVELS	preschool		
PIAGETIAN STAGES	from sensorimotor to preoperations		
ERIKSONIAN STAGES	initiative vs. guilt		
SOCIOEMOTIONAL DEVELOPMENT	egocentric; play experiences with peers; self-expression; conflict and cooperation		
SOCIAL RELATIONSHIPS	seek out those who are developmentally similar, based on equality		
PHYSICAL ATTRIBUTES	become more coordinated; develop preference for one side of body; gain control of gross and fine muscles		
LANGUAGE AND THOUGHT	develop verbal, reading (emergent literacy), and writing skills		
COGNITIVE ABILITIES	tied to present experiences		
SOURCES OF IMPACT ON DEVELOPMENT	home and family		

2. KEY CONCEPTS, PRINCIPLES, AND THEORIES

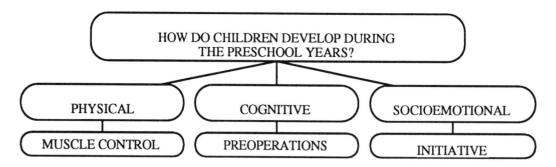

II. WHAT KINDS OF EARLY CHILDHOOD EDUCATION PROGRAMS EXIST?

1. SELF-CHECK ITEM: Describe a day-care center, nursery school, compensatory preschool, and kindergarten. What do research findings suggest about the value of early intervention, compensatory preschool programs, and kindergarten retention? What is meant by developmentally appropriate practice?

TYPICAL RESPONSE: Describe a day care center, nursery school, compensatory preschool, and kindergarten.

day care center	Day care centers exist primarily to provide child-care services for working parents.
nursery school	Like a day care center, nursery schools provide child-care services for working parents; however, a planned program that fosters social and cognitive development (readiness) is provided.
compensatory preschool	These are programs, such as Head Start, that are designed to increase school readiness for preschool children from disadvantaged backgrounds.
kindergarten	Programs for preschoolers that take place one year prior to entry into the first grade. The purpose of kindergarten is to promote social skills.

TYPICAL RESPONSE: What do research findings suggest about the value of early intervention, compensatory readiness training, and kindergarten retention?

early intervention	Several studies show that early intervention programs can have strong effects on students. These effects have lasted into the elementary grades.
compensatory readiness	Research on Head Start programs has generally found positive effects related to children's readiness to enter the elementary grades.
kindergarten retention	Research has shown that, while retention improves children's performance relative to their grademates in the short run, it is detrimental in the long run.

TYPICAL RESPONSE: What is meant by developmentally appropriate practice?

Developmentally appropriate practice is instruction based on students' characteristics and needs, not their ages. Different levels of ability, development, and learning styles are expected, accepted, and used to design curriculum. Developmentally appropriate practice has renewed earlier educational innovations such as non-graded primary and elementary schools, individualized instruction, and learning centers.

2. KEY CONCEPTS, PRINCIPLES, AND THEORIES

III. HOW DO CHILDREN DEVELOP DURING THE ELEMENTARY YEARS?

1. SELF-CHECK ITEM: Continue the comparison chart you began earlier, adding information in each category for middle childhood.

TYPICAL RESPONSE: Continue the comparison chart, adding information about middle childhood.

	EARLY CHILDHOOD	MIDDLE CHILDHOOD	ADOLESCENCE
AGES	three to five	five to twelve	
GRADE LEVELS	preschool	elementary	
PIAGETIAN STAGES	from sensorimotor to preoperations	from preoperations to concrete operations	
ERIKSONIAN STAGES	initiative vs. guilt	industry vs. inferiority	
SOCIO-EMOTIONAL DEVELOPMENT	egocentric; play experiences with peers; self-expression; conflict and cooperation	independent action; cooperation with groups; performing in socially acceptable ways	
SOCIAL RELATIONSHIPS	seek out those who are developmentally similar, based on equality	peers become more important (early on, same-sex relationships)	
PHYSICAL ATTRIBUTES	become more coordinated; develop preference for one side of the body; control of gross and fine muscles	physical development slows; period of adjustment to major changes during preschool years	

LANGUAGE AND THOUGHT	development of verbal, reading (emergent literature), and writing skills	language and thought become more complex
COGNITIVE ABILITIES	tied to present experiences	rapidly developing memory and cognitive skills including ability to think about thinking
SOURCES OF IMPACT ON DEVELOPMENT	home and family	family relationships become less important; peer relationships become more important

2. KEY CONCEPTS, PRINCIPLES, AND THEORIES

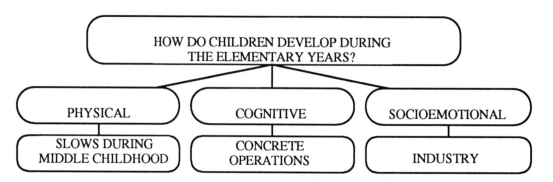

IV. HOW DO CHILDREN DEVELOP DURING THE MIDDLE AND HIGH SCHOOL YEARS?

1. SELF-CHECK ITEM: Add information about adolescence in the last column of your chart, using the same categories as before. Re-read the scenario at the beginning of this chapter, and explain the interaction between Jake and Billy in terms of what you have learned about child development.

TYPICAL RESPONSE: Add information about middle and high school years to your comparison chart. Distinguish between middle childhood and adolescence.

	EARLY CHILDHOOD	MIDDLE CHILDHOOD	ADOLESCENCE
AGES	three to five	five to twelve	twelve to adulthood
GRADE LEVELS	preschool	elementary	middle and secondary
PIAGETIAN STAGES	from sensorimotor to preoperations	from preoperations to concrete operations	from concrete operations to formal operations
ERIKSONIAN STAGES	initiative vs. guilt	industry vs. inferiority	identity vs. role confusion

SOCIO-EMOTIONAL DEVELOPMENT	egocentric; play experiences with peers; self-expression; conflict and cooperation	independent action; cooperation with groups; performing in socially acceptable ways; concern for fairness	appearance of reflectivity; define self; use of intellectual skills that permit consideration of possibilities
SOCIAL RELATIONSHIPS	seek out those who are developmentally similar, based on equality	peers become more important (early on, same-sex relationships)	peers are the focus; friendships, popularity, dating, and sexual relationships important
PHYSICAL ATTRIBUTES	become more coordinated; develop preference for one side of the body; control of muscles	physical development slows; period of adjustment to major changes during the preschool years	onset of puberty; adult-like in appearance
LANGUAGE AND THOUGHT	development of verbal, reading, and writing skills	language and thought become more complex	language and thought become adult-like
COGNITIVE ABILITIES	tied to present experience	rapidly developing memory and cognitive skills including ability to think about thinking	hypothetical-deductive reasoning ability
SOURCES OF IMPACT ON DEVELOPMENT	home and family	family relationships become less important; peers become more important	peers; opposite-sex relationships form

TYPICAL RESPONSE: Explain the interaction between Billy and Jake (scenario at beginning of chapter).

Billy, a first grader, is entering the middle childhood stage of development. Physically, his development is slowing as he adjusts to the major growth spurt of early childhood. He is most likely making the transition from preoperations to concrete operations. In Erikson's terms, he is working on industry issues. He is becoming independent, learning how to cooperate with groups, and focusing on fairness when rules are concerned.

Jake, at 13, is entering adolescence. Physically, he is beginning puberty and is moving away from childhood to adulthood. He is most likely making the transition from concrete operations to formal operations. In Erikson's terms, he is working on identity issues. He is becoming reflective, using intellectual skills that permit him to think about possibilities, and comparing himself to others. Peers and opposite-sex relationships are the focus.

2. KEY CONCEPTS, PRINCIPLES, AND THEORIES

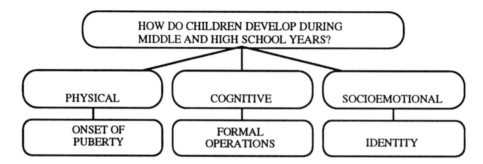

FOR YOUR ENJOYMENT

This section of the study guide includes suggestions for enriching your understanding of a chapter heading you have mastered. You will find information on activities related to the heading and suggestions for research papers, interviews, or presentations.

I. HOW DO CHILDREN DEVELOP DURING THE PRESCHOOL YEARS?

1. Interview or observe a preschool child. Make note of his or her physical, cognitive, and socioemotional development. Compare each with information from the text.

2. For a research topic, review the literature on development of preschoolers.

II. WHAT KINDS OF EARLY CHILDHOOD EDUCATION PROGRAMS EXIST?

1. Interview a day care worker, a nursery school teacher, or a Head Start teacher about the services they provide for children.

2. For a research topic, review the literature on early childhood education and developmentally appropriate practices.

III. HOW DO CHILDREN DEVELOP DURING THE ELEMENTARY YEARS?

1. Interview or observe an elementary school child. Make note of his or her physical, cognitive, and socioemotional development.

2. For a research topic, review the literature on elementary children's development.

IV. HOW DO CHILDREN DEVELOP DURING THE MIDDLE AND HIGH SCHOOL YEARS?

1. Interview or observe an adolescent. Make note of her or his physical, cognitive, and socioemotional development.

2. For a research topic, review the literature on topics related to adolescents.

CHAPTER THREE: SELF-ASSESSMENT

DIRECTIONS: Below are questions related to the main ideas presented in the chapter. Correct answers or typical responses can be found at the end of the study guide.

1. A major accomplishment for preschoolers is

    A. increased control over the large and small muscles.
    B. hypothetical thought.
    C. deductive thinking.
    D. puberty.

2. Which of the following statements about play is false?

    A. Psychologists today generally agree that play is overemphasized in kindergarten and distracts from academics.
    B. Parallel play occurs when children do not interact purposefully with each other to create shared experiences.
    C. Sociodramatic play follows pretend play in the developmental sequence.
    D. Because play is spontaneous and nonreflective, it appears to stimulate creativity.

3. Participation in compensatory preschool programs has been found to

    A. benefit middle class children more than lower class children.
    B. increase disadvantaged children's readiness for kindergarten and first grade.
    C. have stronger effects on long term achievement than on initial achievement.
    D. be of little benefit to children under the age of two.

4. Which of the following cognitive abilities do children usually have when they enter first grade?

    A. They understand abstract concepts.
    B. They know an almost infinite variety of sentences.
    C. They use systematic approaches to solving problems.
    D. They concentrate for long periods of time.

5. During the elementary years, children in middle childhood typically develop all of the following characteristics except

    A. decentered thought.
    B. preoperational thought.
    C. group conformity.
    D. fear of not having a best friend.

6. Which of the following attributes is characteristic of children during the elementary years?

    A. Peers become important.
    B. Reflectivity appears.
    C. Identity issues are central.
    D. Emotional conflicts are experienced.

7. Adolescents who have never experienced an identity crisis because they have prematurely established an identity based on their parents' values and beliefs are in Marcia's

    A. diffusion status.
    B. foreclosure status.
    C. moratorium status.
    D. achievement status.

8. Predictors of dropping out of school include all of the following except

    A. assignment to special education.
    B. poor attendance.
    C. retention.
    D. assistance with academic deficits.

9. Match each developmental challenge below with the period of development in which it is most likely to first occur.

_____ identity diffusion   A. early childhood
_____ friendship
_____ prosocial behavior   B. middle childhood and preadolescence
_____ intimacy
_____ oral language   C. adolescence
_____ sociodramatic play
_____ conflict management

10. Develop an outline for an essay that would begin with the following thesis statement: "Child development has important implications for classroom instruction at each grade level."

PRACTICE TEST ANSWERS

1. True; Physical development during the preschool years involves gaining control over muscle movements.

2. True; During the preschool years, children develop language, reading, and writing skills.

3. Emergent Literacy; Before they begin school, young children have often learned that letters represent sound, that spaces have meaning, and that books have a front and a back.

4. Whole Language; The term whole language is used to refer to a broad range of teaching practices that attempt to move away from the teaching of reading as a set of discrete skills.

5. A; Erikson's initiative vs. guilt stage of socioemotional development begins at about age three and continues until about age six.

6. C; It is projected that by the year 2020 there will be 50 million children in the United states whose primary language is not English.

7. D; Providing at-home services is not suggested as a type of collaborative effort that promotes healthy partnerships between parents and schools.

8. Friendship contributes to healthy socioemotional development as children become aware of the thoughts and the feelings of others, which leads to give-and-take relationships. Prosocial behaviors are voluntary actions toward others such as caring, sharing, comforting, and cooperation—all of which contribute to healthy socioemotional development. Play contributes to development because it promotes new skills and abilities.

9. True; In almost all the countries of the world, children begin their formal schooling at about six years of age.

10. False; There is widespread disagreement regarding schooling practices for children who are under six years of age.

11. B, E, A, C, D; Day care programs provide child care services. Nursery schools are similar to day care programs except they teach "readiness" skills. Compensatory preschool programs, such as Head Start, provide services to children who are disadvantaged. Early intervention programs provide services to infants and to young children who are disadvantaged. Kindergarten programs encourage skill development just prior to first grade.

12. Each child is viewed as a unique person with individual developmental needs. Curriculum and instruction are responsive to individual differences. Children are allowed to move at their own pace in acquiring academic skills. Extensive use is made of projects, play, exploration, group work, and learning centers.

13. False; During the elementary years, physical development slows so that the body can adjust to the changes that occurred during the preschool years.

14. True; Transecents are in transition from childhood to adolescence.

15. True; Between the ages of five and seven, children move from preoperations to concrete operations.

16. C; An important area of personal and social development for elementary school children is self-concept or self-esteem.

17. B; Preadolescents, still depending heavily on their parents, report that they are not understood.

18. Three approaches are power assertion (using punishment), love withdrawal (expressing disapproval), and induction (focusing on why behavior is wrong).

19. Emotional concerns of adolescents include not being accepted into a peer group, not having a best friend, being punished, having parents divorce, not doing well in school, and getting hurt.

20. True; Adolescence is a time of rapid physical and intellectual change, adjustments to the changes, and movement toward adulthood.

21. True; The purpose of puberty is to make individuals capable of reproduction.

22. False; The opposite is true—researchers believe that those who enter puberty early have more difficulty adjusting than do those who enter puberty late.

23. D; According to Piaget, adolescents are moving from concrete operations to formal operations.

24. B; Having students memorize definitions does not necessarily promote hypothetical-deductive thought, which is the ability to consider possibilities.

25. A; Reflectivity is the tendency to think about one's own thinking.

26. B; Erikson calls the experience of not having a sense of one's identity "identity diffusion."

27. Problems associated with adolescence include emotional disorders, drug and alcohol abuse, delinquency and violence, risk of pregnancy, and risk of AIDS.

4
STUDENT DIVERSITY

CHAPTER OVERVIEW

In the previous two chapters, developmental similarities were discussed. The purpose of this chapter is to point out individual differences. Below are some of the ways that student differences affect educational progress.

Diversity in culture can impact student learning.

Diversity in socioeconomic status can affect student learning.

Diversity in ethnicity and race can affect students' school experiences.

Diversity in language can affect student learning.

Diversity in gender can affect students' school experiences

Diversity in intelligence and learning styles can impact student achievement.

CHAPTER OUTLINE

I. WHAT IS THE IMPACT OF CULTURE ON STUDENT LEARNING?

II. HOW DOES SOCIOECONOMIC STATUS AFFECT STUDENT ACHIEVEMENT?
   A. The Role of Child Rearing Practices
   B. The Link Between Income and Summer Learning
   C. The Role of Schools as Middle Class Institutions
   D. School and Community Factors
   E. Is the Low Achievement of Lower Class Children Inevitable?
   F. Implications for Teachers

III. HOW DO ETHNICITY AND RACE AFFECT STUDENTS' SCHOOL EXPERIENCES?
   A. Racial and Ethnic Composition of the United States
   B. Academic Achievement of Minority Group Students
   C. Why Have Minority Group Students Lagged in Achievement?
   D. The Effect of School Desegregation

IV. HOW DO LANGUAGE DIFFERENCES AND BILINGUAL PROGRAMS AFFECT STUDENT ACHIEVEMENT?
   A. Bilingual Education
   B. Effectiveness of Bilingual Programs

V. WHAT IS MULTICULTURAL EDUCATION?
   A. Dimensions of Multicultural Education

VI. HOW DO GENDER AND GENDER BIAS AFFECT STUDENTS' SCHOOL EXPERIENCES?
   A. Do Males and Females Think and Learn Differently?
   B. Sex-Role Stereotyping and Gender Bias

VII. HOW DO STUDENTS DIFFER IN INTELLIGENCE AND LEARNING STYLES?
   A. Definitions of Intelligence
   B. Origins of Intelligence
   C. Theories of Learning Styles
   D. Aptitude Treatment Interactions

PRACTICE TEST

DIRECTIONS: Each chapter heading from the text listed below is followed by a series of related questions worth a total of ten points. Respond to each question, check your answers with those found at the end of the study guide chapter, then determine your score. Consider nine points per heading to be mastery.

For those headings on which you do not score at least nine points, turn to the FOR YOUR INFORMATION section of the study guide for corrective instruction. For those headings on which you do score at least nine points, turn to the FOR YOUR ENJOYMENT section of the study guide for enrichment activities.

I. WHAT IS THE IMPACT OF CULTURE ON STUDENT LEARNING?

True or False

1. (1 point) _____ There is probably as much cultural diversity within the United States as between the United States and other industrialized nations.

2. (1 point) _____ As a nation we tend to be tolerant of cultural differences within our borders.

Short Answer/Essay

3. (3 points) List three aspects of culture absorbed by children by the time they enter school.

_____
_____
_____

4. (5 points) List five ways in which students can differ.

_____
_____
_____
_____
_____

II. HOW DOES SOCIOECONOMIC STATUS AFFECT STUDENT ACHIEVEMENT?

True or False

5. (1 point) _____ Socioeconomic status (SES) refers to an individual's income, occupation, education, and prestige in society as well as race and ethnicity.

6. (1 point) _____ The home environment influences not only academic readiness but also the level of achievement throughout students' careers in school.

7. (1 point) _____ Schools overwhelmingly represent the values and expectations of the middle class.

Multiple Choice

8. (1 point) _____ All of the following child rearing practices for lower or middle socioeconomic status (SES) parents, on average, are true except

A. lower SES parents want success for their children to a greater degree than do middle SES parents.
B. middle SES parents use high quality language when teaching their children.
C. middle SES parents reward their children to a greater degree for intellectual development than do lower SES parents.
D. middle SES parents encourage their children to read or participate in other learning activities.

9. (1 point) _____ Which of the following statements explains why students from backgrounds other than mainstream middle class might have difficulties in school?

A. Schools tend to place importance on individual rather than on group academic achievement.
B. Schools focus on instant gratification.
C. Most classrooms operate on the assumption that cooperation should be valued over competition.
D. Mainstream middle class students have learned to rely on families or on friends for academic support while other groups have not.

Short Answer/Essay

10. (5 points) Explain how community factors impact schools.

_____

_____

_____

_____

_____

III. HOW DO ETHNICITY AND RACE AFFECT STUDENTS' SCHOOL ACHIEVEMENT?

Matching

11. (3 points) _____ primary groups of humans distinguished by form of hair, color of skin or eyes, and stature

_____ groups of humans distinguished by customs, characteristics, language, and common history

_____ group of people who is less in number and different from the dominant group in a nation, region, or community

A. ethnic group

B. minority group

C. racial group

Multiple Choice

12. (1 point) _____ According to the U.S. Census Bureau, which of the following statements about population trends is true?

A. The proportion of non-Latinos is expected to decline in the next 20 years.
B. The proportion of Latinos is expected to decline in the next 20 years.
C. The proportion of Asians is expected to decline by 14 percent by the year 2010.
D. The proportion of African Americans under 25 is expected to grow by 14 percent by the year 2010.

13. (1 point) _____ Prior to 1954, the policy of the U.S. educational system in many states was

A. to desegregate schools.
B. "separate but equal" education for African Americans.
C. to bus students in order to provide multicultural experiences for all students.
D. to create magnet schools in order to overcome segregation laws.

14. (1 point) _____ Which of the following Supreme Court decisions did away with legal school segregation?

A. Engle v. Vitale
B. Mills v. Board of Education of the District of Columbia
C. Nau v. Nichols
D. Brown v. Board of Education of Topeka

15. (4 points)   List four strategies that promote healthy diversity in schools.

_____
_____
_____
_____

IV. HOW DO LANGUAGE DIFFERENCES AND BILINGUAL PROGRAMS AFFECT STUDENT ACHIEVEMENT?

True or False

16. (1 point) _____ In the early 1980s, 13.3 percent of all U.S. children age 5 to 14 were from families in which the primary language spoken was not English.

17. (1 point) _____ Students whose dominant language is not English are more than twice as likely to be performing below grade level than students from similar cultural backgrounds whose dominant language is English.

18. (1 point) _____ "English as a second language" programs are similar in nature and quality to "bilingual education" programs.

Sentence Completion

19. (1 point) _____ is the term used to refer to those students who have not attained an adequate level of English proficiency to succeed in an English-only program.

20. (1 point) _____ is the term used to describe programs for students with limited proficiency in English. It teaches the students in their own language part time while English is also used.

Short Answer/Essay

21. (2 points)   List two arguments in favor of bilingual education.

_____
_____

Short Answer/Essay

22. (3 points)   List three arguments against bilingual education.

_____
_____
_____

V. WHAT IS MULTICULTURAL EDUCATION?

True or False

23. (1 point) _____ Multicultural education encompasses all policies and practices schools use to improve educational outcomes— not only for students of different ethnic, social class, and

religious backgrounds—but also for students of different genders and exceptionalities.

24. (1 point) _____ The first step in multicultural education is for teachers and other school staff to learn about the cultures that make up their student body and to identify possible curriculum bias.

Short Answer/Essay

25. (4 points) List four ways in which a multicultural curriculum can be implemented in classrooms.

_____
_____
_____
_____

26. (4 points) List four questions teachers can ask themselves about how they have made their classrooms culturally sensitive and gender fair.

_____
_____
_____
_____

VI. HOW DO GENDER AND GENDER BIAS AFFECT STUDENTS' SCHOOL EXPERIENCES?

True or False

27. (1 point) _____ All societies treat males differently than females; however, the roles occupied by each across cultures are broad.

28. (1 point) _____ Many of the observed differences between females and males can be linked to early socialization experiences.

Multiple Choice

29. (1 point) _____ All of the following statements regarding gender differences in learning are true except

A. studies generally find that males score higher than females on tests of general knowledge.
B. females tend to score higher on tests of language.
C. there is no gender difference on tests of verbal ability.
D. females tend to score higher on measures of abstract reasoning and memory.

30. (3 points) List three ways in which parents or adults reinforce sex role stereotyping and gender bias.

_____

_____

_____

31. (4 points) List four ways in which teachers reinforce sex role stereotyping and gender bias.

_____

_____

_____

_____

VI. HOW DO STUDENTS DIFFER IN INTELLIGENCE AND LEARNING STYLES?

Sentence Completion

32. (1 point) _____ is the term used to describe a general aptitude for learning, including the ability to deal with abstractions and to solve problems.

33. (1 point) _____ is the term used to represent a single score produced by Alfred Binet's test to represent the broad range of skills assessed by his test.

34. (1 point) _____ Charles Spearman believed that there are variations in an individual's ability across tasks; however, he also believed in a general intelligence factor, which he called ___.

Multiple Choice

35. (1 point) _____ Which of the following statements is true regarding intelligence and schooling?

A. Schooling has little or no effect on intelligence.
B. Intelligence is the primary factor that influences how well a student will perform in school.
C. IQ is not a fixed, unchangeable attribute, but rather is fluid and influenced by environmental factors.
D. What a student knows about a course beforehand (prior knowledge) is probably less important than intelligence.

36. (1 point) _____ Which of the following learning styles reflects the degree to which people perceive stimuli as whole patterns?

A. field dependence
B. field independence
C. impulsivity
D. reflectivity

37. (1 point) _____ Studies that have attempted to match teaching styles to learning styles have

A. only inconsistently found any benefits for learning.
B. demonstrated that learning increases when styles match.
C. shown that learning actually decreases when styles match.
D. found that students like their teachers more when styles are similar.

Short Answer/Essay
38. (4 points) Explain how teachers can accommodate learning styles.

_____

_____

_____

_____

_____

SCORING	POINTS NEEDED FOR MASTERY	POINTS RECEIVED
I. WHAT IS CULTURAL DIVERSITY?	9	
II. HOW DOES SOCIOECONOMIC STATUS AFFECT STUDENT ACHIEVEMENT?	9	
III. HOW DO ETHNICITY AND RACE AFFECT STUDENTS' SCHOOL EXPERIENCES?	9	
IV. HOW DO LANGUAGE DIFFERENCES AND BILINGUAL PROGRAMS AFFECT STUDENT ACHIEVEMENT?	9	
V. HOW DO GENDER AND GENDER BIAS AFFECT STUDENTS' SCHOOL EXPERIENCES?	9	
VI. HOW DO STUDENTS DIFFER IN INTELLIGENCE AND LEARNING STYLES?	9	
VII. WHAT IS MULTICULTURAL EDUCATION?	9	

FOR YOUR INFORMATION

This section of the study guide includes suggestions for further study of the information you have not yet mastered. You will find information on: 1) typical responses to the SELF-CHECK item(s) from the text; and 2) key concepts, principles, and theories addressed in the text chapter.

I. WHAT IS THE IMPACT OF CULTURE ON STUDENT LEARNING?

1. SELF-CHECK ITEM: List as many components of culture as you can think of, and then hypothesize about the impact of each one on teaching and learning.

TYPICAL RESPONSE: List cultural components and hypothesize about the impact.

Culture can be defined as the language, attitudes, ways of behaving, and other aspects of life (dress, values, interests, religion, food preferences, dance, hobbies, hair styles, etc.) that characterize a group of people. All of these aspects can influence student learning. While relatively homogeneous classrooms might be easier to teach (e.g. examples can be culturally relevant to all), the richness of diversity might be missed.

2. KEY CONCEPTS, PRINCIPLES, AND THEORIES

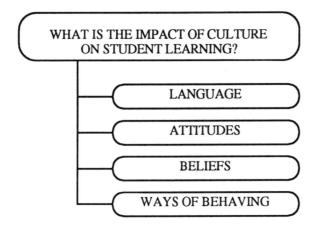

II. HOW DOES SOCIOECONOMIC STATUS AFFECT STUDENT LEARNING?

1. SELF-CHECK ITEM: Summarize the U.S. social class structure. Identify four or more factors related to social class that affect teaching and learning. Give an example of each factor.

TYPICAL RESPONSE: Summarize the U.S. social class structure.

The American social class structure has five groups: upper (3 percent), upper-middle (22 percent), lower-middle (34 percent), upper-working (28 percent), and lower-working (13 percent).

TYPICAL RESPONSE: Identify four social class factors affecting teaching and learning. Give examples.

child rearing practices:	quality of language used by parents with children; activities parents expect of children (e.g., reading)
income:	lower class achievement affected by summer vacations
schools as middle class institutions:	future time orientation and focus on individuality
community factors:	school funding is linked to income of families residing in the district

2. KEY CONCEPTS, PRINCIPLES, AND THEORIES

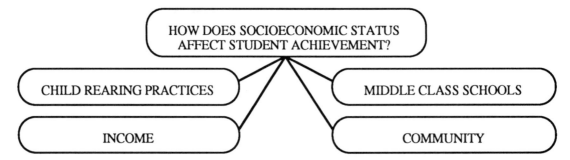

III. HOW DO ETHNICITY AND RACE AFFECT STUDENTS' SCHOOL EXPERIENCES?

1. **SELF-CHECK ITEM:** Define the terms race, ethnic group, and minority group. List cultural, social, economic, and historical factors that account for achievement differences among students. Assess the effectiveness of school desegregation.

TYPICAL RESPONSE: Define race, ethnic group, and minority group.

race:	groups of humans distinguished by form of hair, color of skin and eyes, and stature
ethnic group:	groups of humans distinguished by customs, characteristics, language, and common history
minority group:	group of humans who are less in number and different from the dominant group in a nation, region, or community

TYPICAL RESPONSE: List cultural, social, economic, and historical factors that account for differences.

cultural	social	economic	historical
values	class	economic success	accurate cultural history
language	community status	academic preparation	
parenting styles	expectations	employment record	
family backgrounds	segregation	condition of school	

TYPICAL RESPONSE: Assess the effectiveness of school desegregation.

The overall effect of desegregation on the academic achievement of minority students has been small, though positive. When desegregation begins in elementary school and involves busing minority students to high quality schools, desegregation can have a significant effect on achievement. However, the schools to which minority students are bussed are often no better than the segregated schools they leave behind.

2. KEY CONCEPTS, PRINCIPLES, AND THEORIES

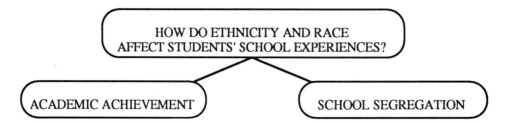

IV. HOW DO LANGUAGE DIFFERENCES AND BILINGUAL PROGRAMS AFFECT STUDENT ACHIEVEMENT?

1. SELF-CHECK ITEM: Define *language minority* and *bilingual education*. Make a chart comparing the many forms bilingual programs can take. According to research, which approaches to bilingual education are most effective? Which are least effective?

TYPICAL RESPONSE: Define language minority and bilingual education and make a chart of the forms bilingual education can take.

language minority:	those individuals whose primary language spoken is not English
bilingual education:	refers to programs for students with limited proficiency in English that teach the students in their own language part of the time while English is being learned
forms of bilingual education:	English as a second language; teach multiple languages to all children; transition programs; English-only classrooms

TYPICAL RESPONSE: According to research, which approaches to bilingual education are most and least effective?

most effective:	Bilingual programs that emphasize culture and language as well as develop and maintain students' self-esteem and pride in both cultures are most effective.
least effective:	Programs that provide nothing more than minimum instruction in English as a second language are least effective.

2. KEY CONCEPTS, PRINCIPLES, AND THEORIES

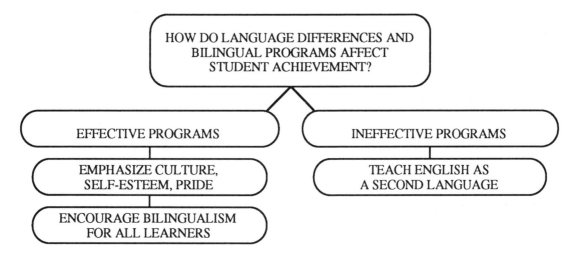

V. WHAT IS MULTICULTURAL EDUCATION?

1. SELF-CHECK ITEM: Define *multicultural education*. List the five key dimensions of multicultural education. Give an example of each. Reread the scenario at the beginning of

this chapter. How should Marva and John proceed? How might multicultural education help the two teachers to resolve their concerns about the Thanksgiving pageant?

TYPICAL RESPONSE: Define multicultural education.

Multicultural education, in its simplest definition, emphasizes the inclusion of non-dominant group perspectives in the curriculum. Another definition lists multicultural education as all policies and practices schools might use to improve education outcomes, not only for students of different ethnic, social class, and religious backgrounds, but also for students of different genders and exceptionalities. A final definition of multicultural education is the idea that all students, regardless of groups to which they belong, should experience educational equality.

TYPICAL RESPONSE: List the key dimensions of multicultural education. Give examples.

content integration	relates to teachers' use of examples, data, and information from a variety of cultures
knowledge construction	refers to teachers helping learners understand how knowledge is created and how it is influenced by race, ethnicity, and social class
prejudice reduction	involves the development of positive relationships among students of different backgrounds and the development of tolerance
equity pedagogy	refers to the use of teaching techniques that facilitate academic success for all learners
empowering school culture	school organization and practices are conducive to the academic and emotional growth of all students

TYPICAL RESPONSE: Reread the case at the beginning of this chapter. How should Marva and John proceed? How might multicultural education help them?

Marva and John should make sure that the Thanksgiving pageant reflects the views of all those involved (perhaps looking at how cultures around the world offer thanks for bountiful harvests).

Marva and John should use resources that are free of stereotypes. Children of different racial or cultural backgrounds can play roles with which they are unfamiliar. For example, Navajo children can be pilgrims and girls can be hunters.

2. KEY CONCEPTS, PRINCIPLES, AND THEORIES

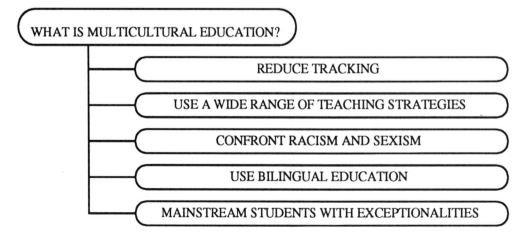

WHAT IS MULTICULTURAL EDUCATION?

REDUCE TRACKING

USE A WIDE RANGE OF TEACHING STRATEGIES

CONFRONT RACISM AND SEXISM

USE BILINGUAL EDUCATION

MAINSTREAM STUDENTS WITH EXCEPTIONALITIES

VI. HOW DO GENDER AND GENDER BIAS AFFECT STUDENTS' SCHOOL EXPERIENCE?

1. SELF-CHECK ITEM: Use research findings to support the view that cultural expectations concerning gender outweigh any actual differences as determinants of student achievement. Give specific examples of gender bias commonly found in the classroom. What can teachers do to avoid gender bias?

TYPICAL RESPONSE: Support the view that cultural expectations and norms concerning gender outweigh real differences as determinants of student achievement.

Cross-cultural research indicates that the sex role is one of the first learned by individuals and that all societies treat males differently from females; therefore, sex role behavior is learned behavior. However, what is considered "natural" behavior for each gender is, in fact, based more on cultural beliefs than on biological necessity. Many of the observed differences between males and females can be clearly linked to differences in early socialization, according to research.

TYPICAL RESPONSE: Give examples of gender bias found in the classroom.

Males engage in more interaction with their teachers in approval, instruction given, and being heard. Teachers tend to punish females more promptly and explicitly for aggressive behavior. Creative behavior of males is rewarded by teachers more often than is creative behavior of females. Textbooks and curriculum promote gender bias (e.g., women's contributions to history are ignored). Teachers and other staff ignore instances of sexual harassment. Teachers tend to choose males to boost their self-esteem and select literature with male protagonists. The contributions of females are largely ignored on standardized tests.

TYPICAL RESPONSE: What can teachers do to avoid gender bias?

Assign classroom jobs without regard to gender. Avoid assigning males as group leaders and females as secretaries. Refrain from using stereotypical behavior statements. Avoid gender teams in competitive activities. Encourage cross-gender collaboration.

2. KEY CONCEPTS, PRINCIPLES, AND THEORIES

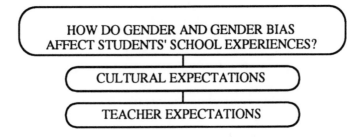

HOW DO GENDER AND GENDER BIAS AFFECT STUDENTS' SCHOOL EXPERIENCES?

CULTURAL EXPECTATIONS

TEACHER EXPECTATIONS

VII. HOW DO STUDENTS DIFFER IN INTELLIGENCE AND LEARNING STYLES?

1. SELF-CHECK ITEM: Define *intelligence*. Discuss present-day understanding of intelligence from a historical perspective. Define *learning styles* and describe traits of field-dependent and field-independent learners.

TYPICAL RESPONSE: Define intelligence. Discuss intelligence from a historical perspective.

Intelligence can be defined as a general aptitude for learning or an ability to acquire and use knowledge or skills. Binet saw intelligence as a single score or intelligence quotient set at 100 for average (50th percentile). Spearman claimed that while there are variations in ability from task to task, there is a general intelligence factor (g) that exists across all learning situations. Sternberg described three types of intellectual ability: intelligence, wisdom, and creativity. Guilford proposed 180 types of intelligences—six of mental operations times five of contents times six of products. Gardner lists eight intelligences: linguistic, musical, spatial, logical-mathematical, bodily-kinesthetic, knowledge of self, understanding of others, and naturalistic.

TYPICAL RESPONSE: Define learning styles and describe traits of field dependent and field independent learners.

Learning styles can be defined as orientations or preferences for approaching learning tasks and processing information. Field dependent individuals tend to see patterns as a whole and tend to have difficulty separating out specific aspects of a situation or pattern. They are more oriented toward people and social relationships and tend to be better at history and literature. Field independent individuals see the parts that make up the large pattern. They prefer problems involving numbers and science.

2. KEY CONCEPTS, PRINCIPLES, AND THEORIES

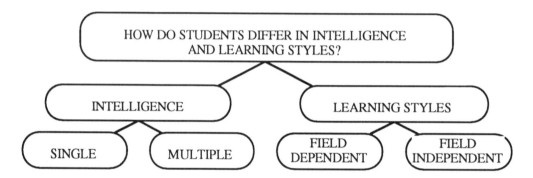

FOR YOUR ENJOYMENT

This section of the study guide includes suggestions for enriching your understanding of a chapter heading you have mastered. You will find information on activities related to the headings and suggestions for research papers, interviews, or presentations.

I. WHAT IS THE IMPACT OF CULTURE ON STUDENT LEARNING?

1. Design a bulletin board or other classroom display that addresses the beliefs, values, or traditions of a culture with which you are unfamiliar.

2. Create a lesson activity (e.g., role play) in which students must experience being a member of some minority group.

II. HOW DOES SOCIOECONOMIC STATUS AFFECT SCHOOL EXPERIENCES?

1. Interview several parents of difference socioeconomic backgrounds. What is their philosophy about education? about child rearing? about the condition of our schools?

2. For a research paper, review the literature on the conditions of urban, suburban, and rural schools.

III. HOW DO ETHNICITY AND RACE AFFECT STUDENTS' SCHOOL EXPERIENCES?

1. For a research paper, review the literature on testing bias related to race.

IV. HOW DO LANGUAGE DIFFERENCES AND BILINGUAL PROGRAMS AFFECT STUDENT ACHIEVEMENT?

1. Debate the question: "Should English become our national language?" List several reasons why and why not.

2. For a research paper, review the literature on educational programs designed to address language differences.

V. WHAT IS MULTICULTURAL EDUCATION?

1. For a research paper, review the related literature on multicultural education.

VI. HOW DO GENDER AND GENDER BIAS AFFECT STUDENTS' SCHOOL EXPERIENCES?

1. Observe a teacher for a few hours or a day. Are there differences related to gender in the ways students are approached, asked questions, disciplined, or rewarded?

2. For a research paper, review the literature on gender differences in schooling.

VII. HOW DO STUDENTS DIFFER IN INTELLIGENCE AND LEARNING STYLES?

1. Create your own learning style profile using the following questions.
    A. What type of atmosphere is best for you when learning?
        1) quiet or some background noise (e.g., music)
        2) warm or cool room temperature
        3) bright or dark room
    B. What type of perceptual information do you prefer?
        1) visual
        2) auditory
        3) tactile, kinesthetic

CHAPTER FOUR: SELF-ASSESSMENT

DIRECTIONS: Below are questions related to the main ideas presented in the chapter. Correct answers or typical responses can be found at the end of the study guide.

1. All of the following are defined as indicators of socioeconomic status except

    A. occupation.
    B. race.

C. income.

D. education.

2. Which of the following terms refers to families whose wage earners are in occupations that are relatively stable but do not require significant higher education?

A. upper class
B. working class
C. lower class
D. middle class

3. The socioeconomic status of various racial and ethnic groups and the groups' scores on standardized tests appear to be

A. positively correlated.
B. negatively correlated.
C. unrelated.

4. What are some specific ways in which cultural differences influence the ways students approach learning tasks?

5. By 2026, what percentage of U.S. students will come from homes in which the primary language is not English?

A. 60
B. 45
C. 25
D. 10

6. Recent referendums about bilingual education in states such as California show that there has been a movement to

A. increase the amount of tax dollars spent on bilingual education.
B. abandon bilingual education in favor of English-only instruction.
C. require all teachers to be proficient in at least two languages.
D. require all students to be bilingual.

7. In a short essay, explain how multicultural education might have been implemented to address the goals of educational and social equality in your own school experience.

8. Studies report all of the following findings except

A. males score higher than females on tests of general knowledge.
B. females score higher than males on language measures.
C. females show more variability in overall academic performance than males.
D. SAT math scores for females are improving.

9. Which of the following statements about gender bias is accurate?

A. Children begin to make gender distinctions after they enter first grade.
B. Males receive more disapproval and blame from teachers than do females.
C. Creativity is rewarded by teachers for females but not for males.
D. Females receive more attention from teachers than do males.

9. Which of the following statements about gender bias is accurate?

   A. Children begin to make gender distinctions after they enter first grade.
   B. Males receive more disapproval and blame from teachers than do females.
   C. Creativity is rewarded by teachers for females but not for males.
   D. Females receive more attention from teachers than do males.

10. Give several definitions of *intelligence*.

PRACTICE TEST ANSWERS

1. True; As much cultural diversity is likely to exist among groups as between groups.

2. False; As a nation, we tend to value characteristics of mainstream, high-status groups and devalue those of other groups.

3. By the time children enter school, they have absorbed many aspects of the culture in which they were raised: language, beliefs, attitudes, ways of behaving, food preferences, and so on.

4. Socioeconomic status, Ethnicity, Race, Language, Gender, Intelligence, Learning style

5. False; Socioeconomic status refers to an individual's income, occupation, education, and prestige, but not his or her race or ethnicity.

6. True; The home environment can influence academic readiness and level of achievement.

7. True; Schools often represent mainstream middle class values.

8. A; The degree to which lower SES parents want success for their children is not higher than middle SES parents.

9. A; Students from lower SES families are less willing to compete and are more interested in cooperation, sometimes viewed as cheating in middle class schools.

10. School funding in most areas of the U.S. is correlated with social class; middle class children are likely to attend schools with greater resources, better paid and better qualified teachers, and other advantages. On top of these differences, schools serving low income neighborhoods may have to spend much more on security, on services for children having difficulties and on many other needs, leaving even less for regular education.

11. C, A, B; A racial group can be defined as one of the primary groups of humans, distinguished by hair form, skin and eye color, and stature. An ethnic group is distinguished by common customs, language, and history. A minority group is a group of people who are less in number than the dominant group.

12. D; African Americans under 25 will grow by 14 percent by the year 2010.

13. B; separate but equal

14. D; Brown vs. the Board of Education of Topeka

15. Strategies for promoting healthy diversity include: be fair, provide equal opportunities for all, eliminate bias, encourage human interaction, use culture/gender fair texts and other curricular materials, assist students in valuing their heritage, avoid resegregation, provide support for language minority students, and use cooperative learning.

16. True; In the early 1980s, 13.3 percent of U.S. school-aged children did not speak English as a primary language.

17. True; When compared to students whose first language is English, students whose primary language is not English are twice as likely to perform below grade level.

18. False; English as a second language programs are not as effective as bilingual programs, which teach students in their own language until they become proficient in English.

19. Limited English Proficient (LEP); refers to language minority students.

20. Bilingual Education; Bilingual programs provide non-English instruction while English is being learned.

21. One argument is that lack of English proficiency is a major reason for academic failure for language minority students. A second argument is that learning a second language facilitates learning in one's own language.

22. One argument against bilingual education is the lack of teachers who are themselves bilingual. Another argument is that students have difficulty with the transition from the bilingual program to the all-English one. A final argument is that the goals of bilingual education sometimes conflict with those of desegregation because they remove students from classes containing English-speaking (often white) students.

23. True; The definition of multicultural education goes beyond culture to encompass ethnic, class, religious, and gender differences.

24. True; Teachers and other school staff must understand diversity by learning about the cultures represented in their schools.

25. The curriculum should represent diverse perspectives, free of race, gender, and handicap stereotypes. It should provide information on contemporary and historical culture that includes more than the dominant view. It should draw on the experiences of the cultures represented by the students. It should allow equal access to all students.

26. Have I made efforts to respect the cultures of my students? Have I allowed students to speak freely? Has the curriculum reflected diversity? Have I avoided segregating students along cultural, gender, or other lines? Have I attempted to understand differences in values, beliefs, and perspectives of all my learners? Have I treated each student with respect?

27. True; Most societies treat females and males differently.

28. True; Many differences between males and females are learned.

29. D; Gender differences do not impact measures of abstract reasoning and memory.

30. From the moment they are born, males and females are viewed differently. After birth, males wear blue while females wear pink. Newborn babies are given sex-appropriate reinforcement and are handled differently. By school age, females are expected to be passive, nurturing, and dependent while males are expected to be more aggressive and independent.

31. Males receive more encouragement for creativity, engage in more interactions

involving approval, instruction giving, and attention by teachers than do females. Females receive punishment more promptly and explicitly by teachers than males.

32. Intelligence; While there are several definitions, most theorists agree that intelligence involves an aptitude for learning.

33. IQ; Intelligence Quotient

34. g; which exists across all learning situations

35. C; Intelligence is not fixed, but rather is influenced by factors such as schooling.

36. A; Field dependent learners tend to see patterns as a whole.

37. A; Studies have been inconclusive.

38. Field dependent learners tend to be more oriented toward people and social relationships, better at recalling conversations and relationships, work best in groups, and prefer history and literature. Field independent learners do well with numbers, science, and problem solving tasks.

5
BEHAVIORAL THEORIES OF LEARNING

CHAPTER OVERVIEW

To this point in the text, development—how individuals change over time—has been the focus. The purpose of this chapter, and the next few that follow, is to consider learning—how individuals use developmental changes to understand their world. In particular, this chapter focuses on behavioral ideas about learning, some of which are listed below.

Behavioral theories of learning consider how individuals react to and interact with the environment.

Behavioral theories of learning evolved from Pavlov's classical conditioning, to Thorndike's law of effect, to Skinner's operant conditioning.

Behavioral theories of learning (operant conditioning) involve principles and schedules of reinforcement.

Behavioral theories of learning include Bandura's observational learning where modeling and vicarious learning are considered.

CHAPTER OUTLINE

I. WHAT IS LEARNING?

II. WHAT BEHAVIORAL LEARNING THEORIES HAVE EVOLVED?
   A. I. Pavlov: Classical Conditioning
   B. E. L. Thorndike: The Law of Effect
   C. B. F. Skinner: Operant Conditioning

III. WHAT ARE SOME PRINCIPLES OF BEHAVIORAL LEARNING?
   A. The Role of Consequence
   B. Reinforcers
   C. Intrinsic and Extrinsic Reinforcers
   D. Punishers
   E. Immediacy of Consequences
   F. Shaping
   G. Extinction
   H. Schedules of Reinforcement
   I . Maintenance
   J. The Role of Antecedents

IV. HOW HAS SOCIAL LEARNING THEORY CONTRIBUTED TO OUR UNDERSTANDING OF HUMAN LEARNING?
    A. Bandura: Modeling and Observational Learning
    B. Meichenbaum's Model of Self-Regulated Learning
    C. Strengths and Limitations of Behavioral Learning Theories

PRACTICE TEST

DIRECTIONS: Each chapter heading from the text listed below is followed by a series of related questions worth a total of ten points. Respond to each question, check your answers with those found at the end of the study guide chapter, then determine your score. Consider nine points per heading to be mastery.

For those headings on which you do not score at least nine points, turn to the FOR YOUR INFORMATION section of the study guide for corrective instruction. For those headings on which you do score at least nine points, turn to the FOR YOUR ENJOYMENT section of the study guide for enrichment activities.

I. WHAT IS LEARNING?

True or False

1. (1 point) _____ Learning is usually defined as a change in an individual caused by experience.

2. (1 point) _____ Learning and development are separate and distinct phenomena.

3. (1 point _____ Learning occurs intentionally or unintentionally.

Multiple Choice

4. (1 point) _____ Which of the following is a definition of learning from a behavioral perspective?

    A. Learning is the unobservable mental process that individuals use to learn and to remember information.
    B. Learning is taking in, processing, storing, and retrieving perceptual information.
    C. Learning is building new knowledge structures upon those previously learned.
    D. Learning includes how pleasurable or how painful consequences of behavior change individuals' behavior over time.

5. (1 point) _____ Which of the following is an example of learning?

    A. An infant cries when frightened.
    B. A student wears a "lucky" shirt during a test.
    C. An adolescent becomes ill after being exposed to influenza.
    D. An athlete is fatigued after a vigorous workout.

6. (5 points)   *Essay/Short Answer*
                    List five things you learned as you read the chapter.

_____

_____

_____

_____

_____

II. WHAT BEHAVIORAL LEARNING THEORIES HAVE EVOLVED?

7. (3 points) _____

Matching
the neutral stimulus becomes the conditioned stimulus that produces a conditioned response

A. preconditioning

B. conditioning

_____
an unconditioned stimulus produces an unconditioned response while a neutral stimulus does not produce a response

C. postconditioning

_____
a neutral stimulus is paired with an unconditioned stimulus that produces an unconditioned response

8. (1 point) _____

Multiple Choice
Which of the following statements best depicts Thorndike's Law of Effect?

A. If an act is followed by a satisfying change in the environment, the chance that the act will be repeated increases.
B. If a previously neutral stimulus is paired with an unconditioned stimulus, the neutral stimulus becomes the conditioned stimulus.
C. Reflexive behaviors account for only a small proportion of all actions.
D. Less desired activities can be increased by linking them to more desired activities.

9. (1 point) _____

Skinner used the term "operant" to refer to

A. behaviors as a response to the environment.
B. stimulus-response (S-R) theory.
C. the law of effect.
D. operating upon the environment in the absence of any known or unknown stimulus.

10. (1 point) _____ Which of the following is an advantage of the Skinner box?

A. It shows that animal learning can be generalized to human learning.
B. It demonstrates the difference between rote and creative learning.
C. It allows for careful scientific study of behavior in a controlled environment.
D. It shows that animals can learn from observing other animals.

Essay/Short Answer

11. (4 point) How are classical conditioning and operant alike and how are they different?

_____

_____

_____

_____

III. WHAT ARE SOME PRINCIPLES OF BEHAVIORAL LEARNING?

Sentence Completion

12. (1 point) _____ are any consequences that strengthen a behavior.

13. (1 point) _____ are reinforcers that satisfy basic human needs.

14. (1 point) _____ are reinforcers that acquire their value by being associated with reinforcers that satisfy basic human needs.

Matching

15. (5 points) _____ increases a behavior by presenting something desired   A. positive reinforcement

_____ decreases a behavior by removing something desired   B. negative reinforcement

_____ decreases a behavior by adding something undesired   C. presentation punishment

_____ eliminates or decreases a behavior by removing its reinforcing agent   D. removal punishment

_____ increases a behavior by removing something undesired   E. extinction

16. (1 point) _____*Multiple Choice*
Which of the following is an example of shaping?

A. anything that is external to the activity, such as praise or good grades
B. a signal as to what behavior(s) will be reinforced or punished
C. the use of small steps combined with feedback to help learners reach goals
D. the linking of less desired activities with more desired ones

17. (1 point) _____ A teacher gives short quizzes over lessons presented at random times during the unit. Which schedule of reinforcement is being depicted in the above scenario?

A. fixed ratio (FR)
B. variable ratio (VR)
C. fixed interval (FI)
D. variable interval (VI)

IV. HOW HAS SOCIAL LEARNING THEORY CONTRIBUTED TO OUR UNDERSTANDING OF HUMAN LEARNING?

Sentence Completion

18. (1 point) _____ is the term used to describe the imitation of others' behavior.

19. (1 point) _____ is the term used to describe the process of learning from others' successes and failures.

Essay/Short Answer

20. (4 points) List the phases of observational learning.

_____
_____
_____
_____

21. (4 points) List the strengths and limitations of behavioral learning theories.

_____
_____
_____
_____

SCORING	POINTS NEEDED FOR MASTERY	POINTS RECEIVED
I. WHAT IS LEARNING?	9	
II. WHAT BEHAVIORAL LEARNING THEORIES HAVE EVOLVED?	9	
III. WHAT ARE SOME PRINCIPLES OF BEHAVIORAL LEARNING?	9	
IV. HOW HAS SOCIAL LEARNING THEORY CONTRIBUTED TO OUR UNDERSTANDING OF HUMAN LEARNING?	9	

FOR YOUR INFORMATION

This section of the study guide includes suggestions for further study of the information you have not yet mastered. You will find information on: 1) typical responses to the SELF-CHECK item(s) from the text; and 2) key concepts, principles, and theories addressed in the text chapter.

I. WHAT IS LEARNING?

1. SELF-CHECK ITEM: List examples of learning. As you read, identify your examples in terms of the kind of learning that takes place, and add new examples.

TYPICAL RESPONSE: List examples and types of learning.

TYPE OF LEARNING	EXAMPLE
classical conditioning	test anxiety, school phobia
operant conditioning	most types of school behaviors
observational learning	observing and modeling a teacher's behaviors

2. KEY CONCEPTS, PRINCIPLES, AND THEORIES

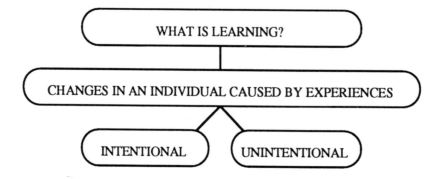

74

II. WHAT BEHAVIORAL LEARNING THEORIES HAVE EVOLVED?

1. SELF-CHECK ITEM: Develop a chart to compare the contributions of Pavlov, Thorndike, and Skinner to our understanding of learning. Label the chart headings Name of Theorist, Name of Theory, Main Concepts, and Research Conducted. Give examples of how the research findings can be applied to classroom learning.

TYPICAL RESPONSE: Develop a chart to compare learning theorists.

THEORIST	THEORY	CONCEPTS	RESEARCH	APPLICATIONS
PAVLOV	classical conditioning	association of a neutral stimulus with an un-conditioned stimulus to produce a conditioned response	focused on observations and careful measurements	few educational applications; test anxiety, school phobia
THORNDIKE	law of effect	if an act is followed by a satisfying change in the environment, the chance that the act will be repeated in similar situations increases	worked with cats that learned how to escape from a box in order to get food	if learning produces satisfaction, more learning will occur
SKINNER	operant conditioning	consequences of one's behavior plays a crucial role in determining one's future behavior	Skinner box: allowed for careful scientific study of behavior in controlled environment	most learning experiences involve operant conditioning

2. KEY CONCEPTS, PRINCIPLES, AND THEORIES

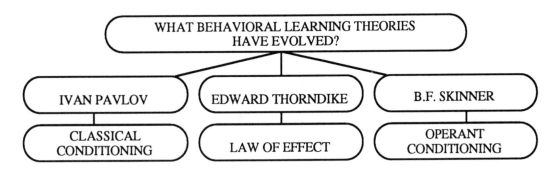

III. WHAT ARE SOME PRINCIPLES OF BEHAVIORAL LEARNING?

1. SELF-CHECK ITEM: List principles of behavioral learning and think of a specific classroom example illustrating each one. Then classify the items in your list in a concept map organized around the headings Consequences, Reinforcement, Punishment, and Antecedent.

TYPICAL RESPONSE: List principles of behavioral theory and give examples.

TERM	DEFINITION	EXAMPLE
primary reinforcer	satisfies basic needs	food, water, security, warmth, sex
secondary reinforcer	a consequence that people learn to value through its relationship with a primary reinforcer	social reinforcers (praise, smiles, hugs, attention), activity reinforcers (toys, games, fun activities), token reinforcers (money, grades, stars, points)
positive reinforcer	presentation of a desired consequence to strengthen a behavior	if they strengthen the behavior, praise, grades, attention
negative reinforcer	release from an undesired consequence to strengthen a behavior	if it strengthens the behavior, a student is released from time out or other isolating situations
Premack principle	using favored activities to reinforce less favored ones	allowing students to go to the library once their work is completed
presentation punishment	presentation of an undesired consequence to weaken a behavior	if they weaken the behavior, scolding, detention, name on board
removal punishment	removal of a desired consequence to weaken a behavior	if they weaken the behavior, time out, loss of privilege
extinction	eliminating a behavior by removing reinforcement	if it eliminates the behavior, ignoring (i.e., neither reinforcing nor punishing the behavior)
shaping	reinforcing small steps with feedback	partial credit for work done that is nearly correct
cueing	information on which behaviors are to be reinforced or punished	telling students that an assignment will be worth ten points
discrimination	use of cues, signals, or information to know when behavior is likely to be reinforced or punished	praising students for correct responses and providing feedback for incorrect responses
generalization	perception of and response to similarities in stimuli	explaining to students that rules in the classroom also apply during lunch and recess

2. KEY CONCEPTS, PRINCIPLES, AND THEORIES

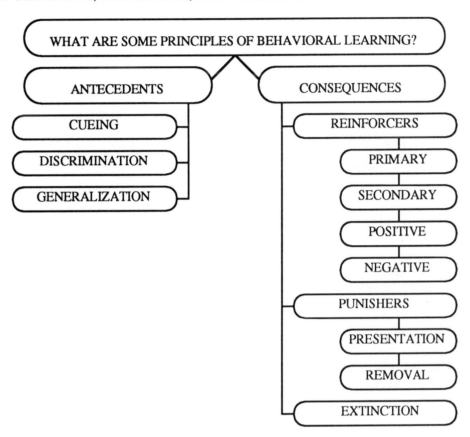

IV. HOW HAS SOCIAL LEARNING THEORY CONTRIBUTED TO OUR UNDERSTANDING OF HUMAN LEARNING?

1. SELF-CHECK ITEM: Extend the comparison chart you began earlier by adding the contributions of social learning theorists as represented by Bandura and Meichenbaum.

TYPICAL RESPONSE: Add social learning theorists to chart.

THEORIST	THEORY	CONCEPTS	RESEARCH	APPLICATIONS
BANDURA	social learning	focus is on effects of cues on behavior and on internal mental processes	observed how consequences of modeling influenced learning	assure attention, model behavior, have students reproduce behaviors, evaluate, motivate
MEICHENBAUM	cognitive behavior modification	focus is on self-instruction and self-regulation	worked on Vygotskian concepts	cognitive model, external guide, self guide

2. KEY CONCEPTS, PRINCIPLES, AND THEORIES

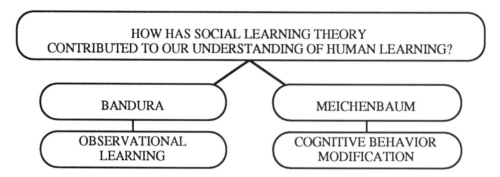

FOR YOUR ENJOYMENT

This section of the study guide includes suggestions for enriching your understanding of a chapter heading you have mastered. You will find information on activities related to the heading and suggestions for research papers, interviews, or presentations.

I. WHAT IS LEARNING?

1. Ask a variety of people to define learning. Analyze the responses to see which ones fit a behavioral definition of learning.

2. For a research paper, review the literature on the history of our understanding about learning through some of the writings of major behavioral (functionalism, associationism) theorists.

II. WHAT BEHAVIORAL LEARNING THEORIES HAVE EVOLVED?

1. For a research paper, review the literature on the history of behaviorism from introspection to physiological psychology, connectionism, and early behaviorism.

III. WHAT ARE SOME PRINCIPLES OF BEHAVIORAL LEARNING?

1. Observe in a classroom for one hour while videotaping the events. Analyze the videotape by listing as many examples of behaviorism in action as you can. Look for some of the following behavioral principles: primary and secondary reinforcers, positive and negative reinforcers, Premack principle, shaping, chaining, extinction, schedules of reinforcement, cueing, discrimination, and generalization.

2. For a research paper, review the literature on the use of behavioral principles in everyday life.

IV. HOW HAS SOCIAL LEARNING THEORY CONTRIBUTED TO OUR UNDERSTANDING OF HUMAN LEARNING?

1. Observe in a classroom. List examples in which students observed a model, then imitated his or her actions.

2. For a research paper, review the literature on observational learning related to TV and to other media violence, for example. Include an explanation of the implications for educators.

CHAPTER FIVE: SELF-ASSESSMENT

DIRECTIONS: Below are questions related to the main ideas presented in the chapter. Correct answers or typical responses can be found at the end of the study guide.

1. Which of the following most clearly represents an example of learning?

    A. Moving one's hand away from a hot object.
    B. Being startled by a loud noise.
    C. Feeling thirsty after exercising.
    D. Having test anxiety.

2. Match the following theories or laws of learning with the theorist most closely associated with each.

_____ classical conditioning	A. Albert Bandura
_____ law of effect	B. Edward Thorndike
_____ operant conditioning	C. Ivan Pavlov
_____ social learning	D. B.F. Skinner

3. An example of a primary reinforcer is

    A. safety or security.
    B. a good grade in school.
    C. money.
    D. praise.

4. What is the Premack Principle? Give two classroom examples.

5. A teacher praises a student for completing a homework assignment with 100 percent accuracy. If the student continues to turn in exceptional assignments, the praise most likely is a

    A. positive reinforcer.
    B. presentation punisher.
    C. removal punisher.
    D. negative reinforcer.

6. Attention, retention, reproduction, and motivation are four phases in

    A. observational learning.
    B. shading.
    C. classical conditioning
    D. reinforcement.

7. Meichenbaum's model for cognitive behavior modification involves all of the following concepts except

    A. self-regulated learning.
    B. private speech.
    C. vicarious learning.
    D. modeling.

8. Which of the following is a limitation of behavioral learning theories?

    A. They compete against cognitive theories of learning.
    B. They attempt to describe learning directly.
    C. They limit the study of learning to observable behaviors.
    D. They rely on faulty research studies to explain learning.

9. Does punishment—for example, reprimands or lost privileges—work well with children? What are some negative effects of punishment? What, according to Skinner, is the best way to deal with good and bad behaviors of students?

10. Explain the differences between classical conditioning and operant conditioning.

PRACTICE TEST ANSWERS

1. True; Learning is a change in behavior caused by experience rather than by innate abilities.

2. False; Learning and development are inseparably linked.

3. True; Sometimes learning is intentional and sometimes it is unintentional.

4. D; From a behavioral perspective, learning focuses on the consequences of behavior change.

5. B; The student "learns" (perhaps from having a positive experience the last time the shirt was worn) that the shirt is lucky.

6. Some things that could be learned include: the definition of learning, that learning can be intentional or unintentional, that Pavlov and Thorndike linked learning to reflexes, that your surroundings are incorporated into what you read, that a lot is known about learning, that the information is useful, etc.

7. C, A, B; During the preconditioning phase, an unconditioned stimulus produces an unconditioned response while a neutral stimulus does not produce a response (UCS produces an UCR); during the conditioning phase, a neutral stimulus is paired with an unconditioned stimulus, which produces an unconditioned response (NS + UCS produces an UCR); and, during the postconditioning phase, the neutral stimulus becomes the conditioned stimulus, which produces a conditioned response (CS produces a CR).

8. A; Thorndike's Law of Effect states that if an act is followed by a satisfying state of affairs, it is likely to be repeated.

9. D; Skinner means "operating" upon the environment.

10. C; According to your text, the Skinner box allows for careful scientific study of behavior in a controlled environment.

11. Classical conditioning shows how learning can affect what was once thought to be involuntary, reflexive behavior. Operant conditioning shows how learning occurs in the absence of any unconditioned stimulus.

12. Reinforcers; increase the frequency of behavior

13. Primary Reinforcers; satisfy basic needs such as food, water, warmth, and sex

14. Secondary Reinforcers; satisfy needs that are associated with primary reinforcers such as money, grades, and praise

15. A, D, C, E, B; Reinforcers increase behavior. Positive reinforcers do so by presenting something desired following a targeted behavior. Negative reinforcers do so by removing something undesired following a targeted behavior. Punishers decrease

behavior. Presentation punishers do so by presenting something undesired following a targeted behavior. Removal punishers do so by removing something desired following a targeted behavior. Extinction, where a behavior stops, occurs when a behavior is neither reinforced nor punished.

16. C; A is an example of extrinsic rewards, B is cueing, and D is the Premack principle.

17. D; Variable interval reinforcement is available at some times, but not at others.

18. Modeling; the imitation of others' behavior

19. Vicarious Learning; learning from the experiences of others' successes or failures

20. Attentional Phase, Retention Phase, Reproduction Phase, and Motivational Phase

21. Behavioral learning theories are firmly established in psychology and have been demonstrated under many different conditions. These principles are useful for explaining much of human behavior; they are even more useful in changing behavior. However, behavioral learning theories are limited in scope as they focus almost exclusively on observable behavior.

6
COGNITIVE THEORIES OF LEARNING: BASIC CONCEPTS

CHAPTER OVERVIEW

In the preceding chapter you were asked to consider learning as behavior. The purpose of this chapter is to consider learning as cognition -- how individuals take in, process, store, and retrieve environmental information. Some main ideas about cognition and learning are listed below.

Cognitive theories of learning use an information processing model that describe the functions of the sensory register, short term memory, and long term memory and explain how each contributes to the processing of information.

Cognitive theories of learning explain the processes of remembering and forgetting.

Cognitive theories of learning demonstrate how to improve memory by using paired-associate learning and serial and free recall learning.

Cognitive theories of learning explain how rote learning and meaningful learning differ.

Cognitive theories of learning describe metacognitive skills used to enhance learning.

Cognitive theories of learning identify effective study strategies that help students learn.

Cognitive theories of learning promote specific teaching strategies that help students learn.

CHAPTER OUTLINE

I. WHAT IS AN INFORMATION PROCESSING MODEL?
   A. Sensory Register
   B. Short Term or Working Memory
   C. Long Term Memory
   D. Factors That Enhance Long Term Memory
   E. Other Information Processing Models

II. WHAT CAUSES PEOPLE TO REMEMBER OR FORGET?
   A. Forgetting and Remembering
   B. Practice

III. HOW CAN MEMORY STRATEGIES BE TAUGHT?
   A. Verbal Learning
   B. Paired-Associated Learning
   C. Serial and Free Recall Learning

IV. WHAT MAKES LEARNING MEANINGFUL?
   A. Rote versus Meaningful Learning
   B. Schema Theory

V. HOW DO METACOGNITIVE SKILLS HELP STUDENTS LEARN?

VI. WHAT STUDY STRATEGIES HELP STUDENTS LEARN?
   A. Note Taking
   B. Underlining
   C. Summarizing
   D. Outlining and Mapping
   E. The PQ4R Method

VII. HOW DO COGNITIVE TEACHING STRATEGIES HELP STUDENTS LEARN?
   A. Making Learning Relevant and Activating Prior Knowledge
   B. Organizing Information

PRACTICE TEST

DIRECTIONS: Each chapter heading from the text listed below is followed by a series of related questions worth a total of ten points. Respond to each question, check your answers with those found at the end of the study guide chapter, then determine your score. Consider nine points per heading to be mastery.

For those headings on which you do not score at least nine points, turn to the FOR YOUR INFORMATION section of the study guide for corrective instruction. For those headings on which you do score at least nine points, turn to the FOR YOUR ENJOYMENT section of the study guide for enrichment activities.

I. WHAT IS AN INFORMATION PROCESSING MODEL?

True or False

1. (1 point) _____ The purpose of the sensory register is to receive large amounts of environmental information.

2. (1 point) _____ Perception of stimuli is more complex than reception of stimuli.

3. (1 point) _____ Attention is the process of focusing on certain stimuli while screening out others.

Sentence Completion

4. (1 point) _____ refers to a storage system that can hold a limited amount of information (five to seven items) for a few seconds.

5. (1 point) _____ refers to a storage system that can hold an unlimited amount of information for long periods of time.

Matching

6. (3 points) _____ type of memory that contains images of experiences organized by when and where they happened   A. semantic

              B. episodic

_____ type of memory that is organized by connected ideas or relationships (schemes)   C. procedural

_____ type of memory that is non-verbal and automatic in its aid to recall things we do well (e.g., reading)

Short Answer/Essay

7. (1 point) Define "levels-of-processing."

_____

_____

8. (1 point) Define "dual code" theory.

_____

_____

II. WHAT CAUSES PEOPLE TO REMEMBER OR FORGET?

True or False

9. (1 point) _____ Most forgetting occurs because information in the sensory register was not transferred to long term memory.

10. (1 point) _____ Interference happens when to-be-measured information gets pushed aside by other information.

Matching

11. (4 points) _____ example: learning to drive on the right side of the road when first taught to drive on the left   A. retroactive inhibition

              B. proactive inhibition

_____ example: when knowing a first language helps to learn a second

              C. proactive facilitation

_____ example: when learning a second language increases awareness of one's native language

              D. retroactive facilitation

_____ example: having no trouble recognizing the letter *b* until the letter *d* is introduced

12. (1 point) _____

Sentence Completion

refer to the effects when learning lists. People tend to remember the first things and the last things.

13. (3 points)

Short Answer/Essay

Give an example of each of the following methods of practice: massed practice, distributed practice, and part learning.

_____

_____

_____

III. HOW CAN MEMORY STRATEGIES BE TAUGHT?

14. (1 point) _____

True or False

Students often learn things as facts before they understand them as concepts or skills.

15. (3 points)

Short Answer/Essay

List three examples of paired-associate learning.

_____

_____

_____

16. (3 points)

List three examples of serial learning.

_____

_____

_____

17. (3 points)

List three examples of free-recall learning.

_____

_____

_____

IV. WHAT MAKES INFORMATION MEANINGFUL?

18. (1 point) _____

Multiple Choice

Which of the following statements is true regarding meaningful learning?

A. We have limited ability to recall meaningful information; however, we can retain rote information far more easily.
B. Mnemonic strategies are necessary for recall of meaningful information.
C. Meaningful learning refers to the memorization of facts or associations.
D. Meaningful learning is not arbitrary and it relates to information or concepts learners already possess.

19. (1 point) _____ Learned information that can be applied only to a restricted, often artificial, set of circumstances is called

    A. rote knowledge.
    B. declarative knowledge.
    C. inert knowledge.
    D. procedural knowledge.

20. (1 point) _____ Which of the following explains how knowledge is stored in memory?

    A. It is thought to be stored in hierarchies.
    B. Information enters and is stored in a random fashion.
    C. It is thought to be stored as an outline.
    D. Information that is most important is stored first and less important information follows.

Short Answer/Essay
21. (2 points) Give two examples of rote learning.

_____

_____

22. (2 points) Give two examples of meaningful learning.

_____

_____

23. (3 points) Explain the requirements necessary for meaningful learning to occur.

_____

_____

_____

V. HOW DO METACOGNITIVE SKILLS HELP STUDENTS LEARN?

Sentence Completion
24. (1 point) _____ is the term used to refer to thinking about one's own thinking.

Multiple Choice
25. (1 point) _____ Which of the following is an example of a metacognitive skill?

    A. recalling a name
    B. listening to a lecture
    C. planning an effective study strategy
    D. reading a poem aloud

26. (1 point) _____ Which of the following statements about metacognition is accurate?

A. While most students do gradually develop adequate metacognitive skills, others do not.
B. Although students develop metacognitive skills at different times, all eventually learn them.
C. Looking for common elements in a given task is an ineffective study strategy.
D. Self-talk hinders learning.

Short Answer/Essay
27. (7 points) Make a list of metacognitive skills used by students in a variety of subjects.

_____
_____
_____
_____
_____
_____

VI.   WHAT STUDY STRATEGIES HELP STUDENTS LEARN?

True or False
28. (1 point) _____ Research on the effectiveness of note taking has been inconsistent.

29. (1 point) _____ Summarization involves writing lengthy statements about all of the ideas presented in a text.

Sentence Completion
30. (1 point) _____ is a study strategy in which main points of the material are presented in a hierarchical format, with each detail organized under a higher-level category.

31. (1 point) _____ is a study strategy in which main ideas are connected using a network-type diagram.

Short Answer/Essay
32. (6 points) List the six steps of the PQ4R method.

_____
_____
_____
_____
_____

VII. HOW DO COGNITIVE TEACHING STRATEGIES HELP STUDENTS LEARN?

Matching

33. (5 points) _____ strategy using examples that are, in one respect, similar, but otherwise, unlike

A. advance organizer

_____ strategy linking prior knowledge to new information by thinking about it in a new way

B. analogy

C. conceptual model

_____ strategy using a diagram to show how concepts are related to each other

D. elaboration

_____ strategy in which the learning process is halted in order to assess learning

E. questioning

_____ strategy presenting a framework to the content prior to the learning experience

Short Answer/Essay

34. (3 points) Give three examples of strategies that enhance understanding and retention by activating prior knowledge.

_____

_____

_____

35. (2 points) List two appropriate ways in which analogies can be used effectively.

_____

_____

SCORING	POINTS NEEDED FOR MASTERY	POINTS RECEIVED
I. WHAT IS AN INFORMATION PROCESSING MODEL?	9	
II. WHAT CAUSES PEOPLE TO REMEMBER OR FORGET?	9	
III. HOW CAN MEMORY STRATEGIES BE TAUGHT?	9	
IV. WHAT MAKES INFORMATION MEANINGFUL?	9	
V. HOW DO METACOGNITIVE SKILLS HELP STUDENTS LEARN?	9	
VI. WHAT STUDY STRATEGIES HELP STUDENTS LEARN?	9	
VII. HOW DO COGNITIVE TEACHING STRATEGIES HELP STUDENTS LEARN?	9	

FOR YOUR INFORMATION

This section of the study guide includes suggestions for further study of the information you have not yet mastered. You will find information on: 1) typical responses to the SELF-CHECK item(s) from the text; and 2) key concepts, principles, and theories addressed in the text chapter.

I. WHAT IS AN INFORMATION PROCESSING MODEL?

1. SELF-CHECK ITEM: Draw a diagram representing the Atkinson-Shiffrin information-processing model that includes the following terms: sensory register, attention, short term (working) memory, rehearsal, repetition, coding, long term (permanent) memory, and retrieval. Using one specific example, explain how information is processed in memory.

TYPICAL RESPONSE: Draw an information processing model.

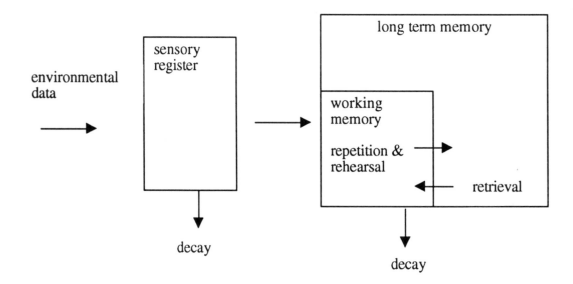

TYPICAL RESPONSE: Using one specific example throughout, briefly explain how information is processed.

Example: learning a new phone number	
environmental stimuli	reading the number in the phone book (visual environmental stimuli)
sensory store	If the phone number is attended to, it will enter the memory system while other phone numbers on the page decay through inattention.
short term memory	If the phone number is to be remembered for a brief period of time, repetition of the number—saying it over and over again—will keep it available. Once the number is dialed, it decays.

long term memory   If the phone number is to be remembered so that it can be retrieved at a later
time, then further processing is necessary (e.g., rehearsal, elaboration,
or organization of the information). Forgetting is the inability to
search and find stored information.

2. KEY CONCEPTS, PRINCIPLES, AND THEORIES

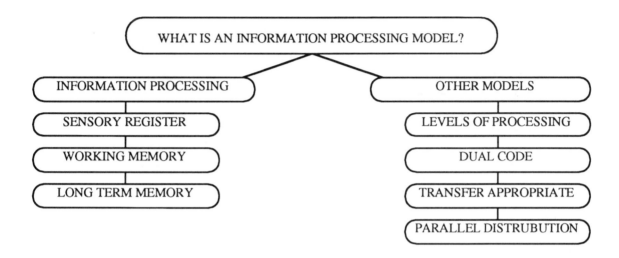

II. WHAT CAUSES PEOPLE TO REMEMBER OR FORGET?

1. SELF-CHECK ITEM: Reread the vignette at the beginning of this chapter on Ms.
Bishop's memory experiment. Why did her students remember some things and not
others? How might different kinds of practice enhance the students' learning in this case?

TYPICAL RESPONSE: In the scenario, why did students forget? Why did they remember? What
strategies can enhance learning?

One possible explanation for forgetting is that the students did not transfer information about the
diagram from short term memory to long term memory so that it could be retrieved during the discussion.
Another possible explanation for forgetting is that the amount of information being asked to remember
exceeded short term memory capacity.

One possible solution for remembering is that if students had a similar learning experience, they
perhaps used it to facilitate their new learning experience. Another explanation is that some
information was more salient than other information. For example, colors might be remembered more
easily than text.

Practice strategies that enhance memory include distributed practice, part learning, overlearning, and
enactment.

2. KEY PRINCIPLES, CONCEPTS, AND THEORIES

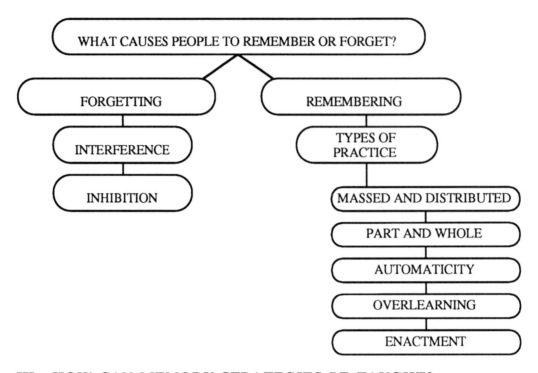

III. HOW CAN MEMORY STRATEGIES BE TAUGHT?

1. SELF-CHECK ITEM: Draw a diagram of the memory strategies associated with paired-associate learning, serial learning, and free-recall learning.

TYPICAL RESPONSE: Draw a diagram of memory strategies.

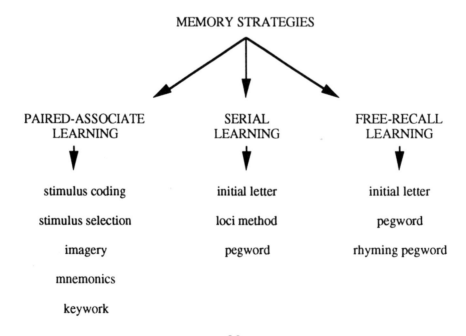

2. KEY CONCEPTS, PRINCIPLES, AND THEORIES

See 1: SELF-CHECK ITEM above.

VI. WHAT MAKES INFORMATION MEANINGFUL?

1. SELF-CHECK ITEM: Explain the difference between rote and meaningful learning, the role of schemes in learning, and the importance of prior knowledge in learning. Create a chart showing examples of rote learning and meaningful learning.

TYPICAL RESPONSE: Explain rote and meaningful learning, the role of schemes in learning, and the importance of prior knowledge in learning.

> Rote and meaningful learning differ in that rote learning refers to the memorization of facts or associations while meaningful learning refers to the non-arbitrary relationship between new information and prior knowledge. The role of schemes in learning is that as we learn new information or add to existing knowledge, we categorize, elaborate, and organize it in a way we find meaningful. Prior knowledge facilitates new learning by meshing the two to bring a deeper understanding to each.

TYPICAL RESPONSE: Give three examples of rote and meaningful learning.

ROTE LEARNING	MEANINGFUL LEARNING
memorizing that 2/4 = 1/2	understanding that eating 2/4 of a cake is the same as eating 1/2 of a cake
memorizing the bones and muscles of the body	understanding that the muscular system and the skeletal system work together to create movement
memorizing the steps necessary for performing cardiopulmonary resuscitation (CPR)	understanding when cardiopulmonary resuscitation (CPR) is necessary and when it is not

2. KEY CONCEPTS, PRINCIPLES, AND THEORIES

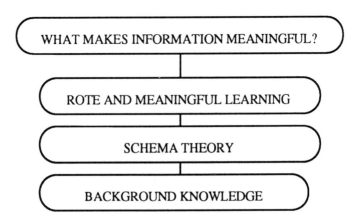

WHAT MAKES INFORMATION MEANINGFUL?

ROTE AND MEANINGFUL LEARNING

SCHEMA THEORY

BACKGROUND KNOWLEDGE

IV. HOW DO METACOGNITIVE SKILLS HELP STUDENTS LEARN?

1. SELF-CHECK ITEM: Define metacognition and explain how self-questions promote learning.

TYPICAL RESPONSE: Define metacognition and explain how self-questions promote learning.

> Metacognition means knowledge about one's own learning or knowledge of how to learn. For reading activities, students comprehend better if they ask themselves who, what, where, and how questions as they read. For writing activities, students do better if they ask "For whom am I writing? What is being explained? What are the steps?" And, students do better in math if they talk themselves through problem solving.

2. KEY CONCEPTS, PRINCIPLES AND THEORIES

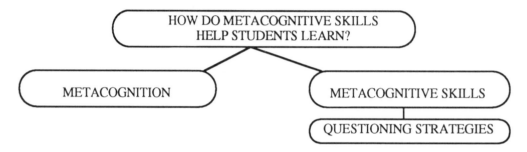

IV. WHAT STUDY STRATEGIES HELP STUDENTS LEARN?

1. SELF-CHECK ITEM: Make a list of all the study strategies listed in this section. Provide a plan showing how each strategy is taught.

TYPICAL RESPONSE: List study strategies and plan steps for teaching each.

STUDY STRATEGY	TEACHING PLAN
underlining	assist student in selecting key words, phrases, or concepts
outlining	have students follow headings and subheadings of the text
summarizing	have students read a paragraph of text, then put into their own words
mapping	have students draw a concept map of a topic that is hierarchical in structure
PQ4R	Prior to reading a chapter, have students preview by skimming through the material and asking questions about concepts they might encounter. Next, have students read and, while reading, reflect, recite, and review the material.

2. KEY CONCEPTS, PRINCIPLES, AND THEORIES

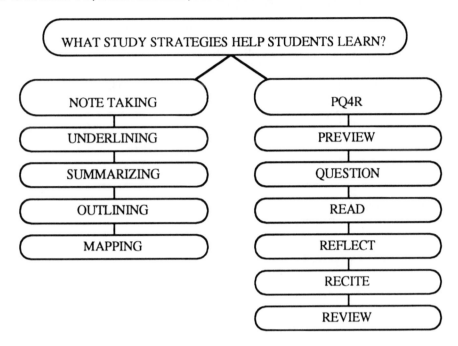

VI. HOW DO COGNITIVE TEACHING STRATEGIES HELP STUDENTS LEARN?

1. SELF-CHECK ITEM: Compare cognitive teaching strategies that help students to elicit prior knowledge with cognitive teaching strategies that assist the learner in organizing new learned information. Give an example of how each strategy can be used in the classroom.

TYPICAL RESPONSE: Compare strategies and give an example of each.

Advance organizers, analogies, and elaboration strategies activate the learner's prior knowledge before a lesson is presented. Questioning and conceptual models assist the learner in organizing newly learned information.

LESSON STRATEGY	EXAMPLE
advance organizer	initial statement about a subject to be learned that provides structure to the new information and relates it to information students already possess
analogy	using an example that is like the concept to be learned on one level, but unlike the concept on others
elaboration	provide a process of thinking about material to be learned in a way that connects it to information or ideas already in the learner's mind
questioning	procedure that allows students to stop instruction in order to assess their learning of the material to that point
conceptual model	an introduction of diagrams showing how elements or concepts are related

2. KEY CONCEPTS, PRINCIPLES, AND THEORIES

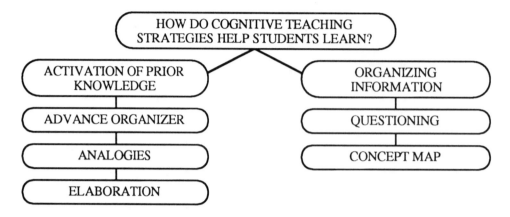

FOR YOUR ENJOYMENT

This section of the study guide includes suggestions for enriching your understanding of a chapter heading you have mastered. You will find information on activities related to the heading and suggestions for research papers, interviews, or presentations.

I. WHAT IS AN INFORMATION PROCESSING MODEL?

1. Interview several individuals about how they remember (e.g., study for an exam). Try to examine the responses from an information processing perspective.

2. For a research paper, review the research on the relationship between computers and human learning.

II. WHAT CAUSES PEOPLE TO REMEMBER OR FORGET?

1. Create a lesson plan that addresses practice; distributed, part, or enactment.

III. HOW CAN MEMORY STRATEGIES BE TAUGHT?

1. Design a lesson that requires memorization of information. Include a strategy that will enhance recall.

2. For a research paper, review the literature on memory enhancement.

IV. WHAT MAKES LEARNING MEANINGFUL?

1. Analyze a lesson from a teacher's manual. Consider the prior knowledge (e.g., facts, concepts) necessary for understanding the lesson.

2. For a research paper, review the literature on prior knowledge and its effects on new learning.

V. HOW DO METACOGNITIVE SKILLS HELP STUDENTS LEARN?

1. Select students who are at the grade level you intend to teach and interview them about their learning strategies. Analyze their responses.

VI. WHAT STUDY STRATEGIES HELP STUDENTS LEARN?

1. Interview various individuals on how they study. According to research, are their strategies useful?

2. For a research paper, review the literature on the PQ4R study strategy.

VII. HOW DO COGNITIVE TEACHING STRATEGIES HELP STUDENTS LEARN?

1. For your area, design some study skill strategies that would be helpful to your students.

CHAPTER SIX: SELF-ASSESSMENT

DIRECTIONS: Below are questions related to the main ideas presented in the chapter. Correct answers or typical responses can be found at the end of the study guide.

1. Sperling's study involving the recall of 12 letters projected briefly on a screen illustrates the limitations of which of the following memory areas?

A. long term memory
B. short term memory
C. external environment
D. the sensory register

2. Match the following memory types of memory with its definition.

_____ part of long term memory that stores images of personal experiences

_____ mental networks of related concepts associated with new information

_____ type of memory associated with automaticity

A. procedural memory

B. episodic memory

C. semantic memory

3. Which of the following teaching strategies would be least effective in reducing retroactive inhibition?

A. Be consistent in the methods used when teaching similar concepts.
B. Teach one concept thoroughly before introducing another.
C. Use mnemonic devices to point out differences between concepts.
D. Teach concepts at different times, such as in separate class periods.

4. Provide an example of how someone develops automaticity.

5. Match each type of verbal learning skill with its example.

_____ learning U.S. states and capitals   A. free-recall learning

_____ memorizing the order of planets   B. paired-associate learning

_____ learning about major organs of the body   C. serial learning

6. Give several examples of mnemonics.

7. Which of the following study strategies is associated with note-taking?

A. outlining and mapping
B. PQ4R method
C. loci method
D. pegword method

8. What is the name given to the prelearning activities and techniques that orient students to new material?

A. PQ4R method
B. metacognition
C. advance organizers
D. keyword method

9. Give three examples of how a teacher can make learning relevant to students by activating prior knowledge.

10. How does organizing information enhance learning?

PRACTICE TEST ANSWERS

1. True; The sensory register receives large amounts of information from the senses and holds it for a very short time, no more than a couple of seconds. If nothing happens to the information, it is lost.

2. True; Perception is not as straightforward as reception of stimuli; rather, it is influenced by our mental state, past experiences and knowledge, motivation, and many other factors.

3. True; Attention refers to shifting priorities so that irrelevant stimuli are screened out.

4. Short term memory; Short term memory is a processing system that holds a limited amount of information for a few seconds (without repetition or rehearsal).

5. Long term memory; Long term memory is a storage system that can hold an unlimited amount of information over long periods of time.

6. B, A, C; Episodic memory stores images of events, semantic (or declarative) memory stores information of ideas, facts, or relationships, and procedural memory is a compilation of semantic information that has become automatic and non-verbal, thus requiring little processing time or space.

7. Levels of processing theory holds that people subject stimuli to different levels of mental manipulation. Only information subjected to deep level processing is retained.

8. Dual code theory hypothesizes that information that is retained in long term memory in two forms—episodic and semantic—is recalled more easily than information stored in one form exclusively.

9. False; Most forgetting occurs because information in short term memory is not transferred to long term memory.

10. True; Short term memory is limited in its capacity; therefore, attention to one mental task can interfere with attention to another through overloading.

11. B, C, D, A; Proactive inhibition occurs when the learning of one set of information interferes with learning of later information. Proactive facilitation occurs when learning one thing can help in learning similar, but new, information. Retroactive facilitation occurs when learning new information improves one's understanding of previously learned information. Retroactive inhibition occurs when previously learned information is lost because it is mixed up with new and somewhat similar information.

12. Primacy and recency; The tendency to learn the first things presented is called the primacy effect. The tendency to learn the last things presented is called the recency effect.

13. An example of massed practice would be "cramming" for an exam—practicing newly learned information intensively in a short span of time. An example of distributed practice would be homework—practicing newly learned information over an extended span of time. An example of part learning would be learning multiplication tables by 2s, then 3s, then 4s over time—practicing information that is broken down into parts.

14. True; Students often learn things as facts before they understand concepts or skills.

15. Imagery, stimulus selection and coding, and mnemonics

16. Loci method, pegword method, initial letter

17. Rhyming pegwords, songs, catchy phrases, initial letter strategies

18. D; Meaningful learning involves the use of old information in a non-arbitrary fashion.

19. C; Knowledge that could and should be applicable to a wide range of situations, but is only applied to a restricted set of circumstances, is called inert knowledge.

20. A; According to schema theory, information is stored in hierarchies.

21. Memorizing multiplication tables, chemical symbols for the elements, words in a foreign language, and names of the bones and muscles of the body

22. Understanding that silver is an excellent conductor of electricity—and that silver and electricity have a relationship.

23. Meaningful learning requires the active involvement of the learner who has a history of prior experiences and knowledge (background knowledge) to bring to understanding and incorporating new information.

24. Metacognition; Metacognition means knowing about one's way of learning.

25. C; Thinking skills and study skills (e.g., planning a study strategy) are metacognitive skills.

26. A; Not all students develop metacognitive skills.

27. All of the following are examples of metacognitive skills: assessing understanding, figuring out length of study time, choosing a study plan, looking for common elements in a given task, questioning, and self-talk.

28. True; Note taking research is inconsistent; however, it seems to work best with complex, conceptual materials in which the critical task is to identify main ideas.

29. False; Summarizing involves writing brief statements that represent the main ideas being read.

30. Outlining; Outlining presents the main points of the material in a hierarchical format, with each detail organized under a higher level category.

31. Mapping; Networking identifies main ideas and then makes connections between them in the form of a diagram.

32. The steps of the PQ4R method are: 1) preview; 2) question; 3) read; 4) reflect on the material; 5) recite; and 6) review.

33. B, D, C, E, A; Analogies are examples that are alike in one aspect, but otherwise

different. Elaboration means the linking of new information with prior knowledge by adding relevant or irrelevant connections. Conceptual models are diagrams showing relationships between concepts. Questioning gives students the chance to assess their understanding during the learning process. Advance organizers provide a framework for the to-be-learned material.

34. Three strategies would include: 1) using advance organizers; 2) having students discuss what they already know about the topic; and 3) asking students to predict outcomes.

35. Analogies work best when they are different from the process being explained and when the analogy is thoroughly familiar to the learner.

7
EFFECTIVE INSTRUCTION

CHAPTER OVERVIEW

The purpose of this chapter is to discuss several research-based instructional strategies that are effective in promoting student achievement. Several methods and strategies are described below.

Effective instruction includes direct instruction teaching approaches that emphasize teacher control over classroom events, including lesson presentation.

Effective instruction, from a direct instruction approach, consists of several parts including a statement of the objective(s), review of the prerequisites, presentation of the material, solicitation of student responses through guided and independent practice, assessment of performance, and distributed practice.

Effective instruction, from a direct instruction approach, has advantages and disadvantages when compared with other instructional methods.

Effective instruction methods help students learn and transfer concepts.

Effective instruction makes use of whole group and small group discussion strategies.

CHAPTER OUTLINE

I. WHAT IS DIRECT INSTRUCTION?

II. HOW IS A DIRECT INSTRUCTION LESSON TAUGHT?
    A. State Learning Objectives
    B. Orient Students to the Lesson
    C. Review Prerequisites
    D. Present New Material
    E. Conduct Learning Probes
    F. Provide Independent Practice
    G. Assess Performance and Provide Feedback
    H. Provide Distributed Practice and Review

III. WHAT DOES RESEARCH ON DIRECT INSTRUCTION METHODS SUGGEST?
    A. Advantages and Limitations of Direct Instruction

IV. HOW DO STUDENTS LEARN AND TRANSFER CONCEPTS?
    A. Concept Learning and Teaching
    B. Teaching for Transfer of Learning

V. HOW ARE DISCUSSIONS USED IN INSTRUCTION?
    A. Subjective and Controversial Subjects
    B. Difficult and Novel Concepts
    C. Affective Objectives
    D. Whole Class Discussion
    E. Small Group Discussion

PRACTICE TEST

DIRECTIONS: Each chapter heading from the text listed below is followed by a series of related questions worth a total of ten points. Respond to each question, check your answers with those found at the end of the study guide chapter, then determine your score. Consider nine points per heading to be mastery.

For those headings on which you do not score at least nine points, turn to the FOR YOUR INFORMATION section of the study guide for corrective instruction. For those headings on which you do score at least nine points, turn to the FOR YOUR ENJOYMENT section of the study guide for enrichment activities.

I. WHAT IS DIRECT INSTRUCTION?

True and False

1. (1 point) _____ The term "direct instruction" is used to describe lessons in which the teacher transmits information directly to students, structuring class time to reach a clearly defined set of objectives as efficiently as possible.

2. (1 point) _____ Direct instruction is appropriate when exploration, discovery, and open-ended objectives drive the lesson.

3. (1 point) _____ There is a general agreement among researchers and teachers as to the sequence of events that characterize effective direct instruction lessons.

Short Answer/Essay

4. (7 points) Describe the parts of a direct instruction model.

_____

_____

_____

II. HOW IS A DIRECT INSTRUCTION LESSON TAUGHT?

True or False

5. (1 point) _____ The sequence of activities included in an effective lesson varies according to the grade level of the students.

6. (1 point) _____ The sequence of activities included in an effective lesson varies according to the subject matter content.

7. (8 points)   *Order in Sequence*
_____ Provide distributed practice.
_____ Review prerequisites.
_____ Conduct learning probes.
_____ State learning objective(s).
_____ Provide independent practice.
_____ Present new material.
_____ Assess performance and provide feedback.
_____ Orient students to lesson.

III. WHAT DOES RESEARCH ON DIRECT INSTRUCTION METHODS SUGGEST?

Sentence Completion

8. (1 point)   _____ are direct instruction models based on the practices of the most effective teachers.

9. (1 point)   _____ are direct instruction models based on well-structured and highly organized planning, including the motivation of students and the management of classrooms.

10. (1 point)   _____ is the term used by Madeline Hunter to describe a method for stimulating students' interest.

Multiple Choice

11. (1 point)   _____ Research on Madeline Hunter's mastery teaching program suggests that it is

A. superior to other direct instruction programs at all grade levels and across disciplines.
B. no more and no less effective than other direct instruction programs.
C. inferior to other direct instruction programs.

12. (1 point)   _____ Which of the following research findings is accurate regarding the systematic instruction program called DISTAR?

A. DISTAR was least effective in increasing students' reading and math achievement when compared to other systematic instruction models.
B. DISTAR increased students' academic achievement, but had no effect on students' self-esteem.
C. DISTAR brought low achieving, disadvantaged students to nearly average.

Short Answer/Essay

13. (2 points)   List two advantages of direct instruction.

14. (3 points)   List three limitations of direct instruction.

_____

_____

_____

IV. HOW DO STUDENTS LEARN AND TRANSFER CONCEPTS?

True or False

15. (1 point) _____ A concept is a category under which specific elements may be grouped.

16. (1 point) _____ With a rule-example-rule approach to concept learning, teachers give students instances of the concept, then ask them to provide a definition.

17. (1 point) _____ Transfer of learning depends on the degree of similarity between the learning situation and the situation to which it is to be applied.

18. (1 point) _____ If a student learns a skill or concept in one domain, it can be assumed that the knowledge will transfer to another domain.

Short Answer/Essay

19. (3 points)   List the three rules to follow when presenting examples of concepts.

_____

_____

_____

20. (3 points)   Describe the difference in strategies between teaching for transfer and teaching initial learning.

_____

_____

_____

V. HOW ARE DISCUSSIONS USED IN INSTRUCTION?

Short Answer/Essay

21. (3 points)   List three types of learning objectives that are best met by using discussions.

_____

_____

_____

22. (1 point)   Define "inquiry oriented discussion."

_____

23. (1 point)   Define "exploring points of view."

_____

24. (2 points)   List two functions of the teacher when using whole class discussion.

_____

_____

25. (3 points)   Explain the roles of the teacher, the group leader, and the group secretary when using small group discussion.

_____

_____

_____

SCORING	POINTS NEEDED FOR MASTERY	POINTS RECEIVED
I. WHAT IS DIRECT INSTRUCTION?	9	
II. HOW IS A DIRECT INSTRUCTION LESSON TAUGHT?	9	
III. WHAT DOES RESEARCH ON DIRECT INSTRUCTION SUGGEST?	9	
IV. HOW DO STUDENTS LEARN AND TRANSFER CONCEPTS?	9	
V. HOW ARE DISCUSSIONS USED IN INSTRUCTION?	9	

FOR YOUR INFORMATION

This section of the study guide includes suggestions for further study of the information you have not yet mastered. You will find information on: 1) typical responses to the SELF-CHECK item(s) from the text; and 2) key concepts, principles, and theories addressed in the text chapter.

I. WHAT IS DIRECT INSTRUCTION?

1. SELF-CHECK ITEM: List the sequence of steps that characterize a direct instruction lesson.

TYPICAL RESPONSE: List the steps in a direction instruction lesson.

1. State the learning objective and orient students to the lesson.
2. Review the prerequisites.
3. Present new material.

4. Conduct learning probes.
5. Provide independent practice.
6. Assess students' performance and provide feedback.
7. Provide distributed practice and review.

2. KEY CONCEPTS, PRINCIPLES, AND THEORIES

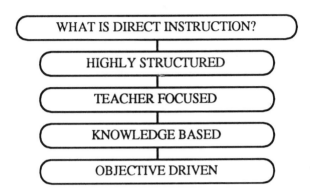

II. HOW IS A DIRECT INSTRUCTION LESSON TAUGHT?

1. SELF-CHECK ITEM: What is the purpose of each step of a direct instruction model? List strategies and provide examples for each of the seven steps.

TYPICAL RESPONSE: What is the purpose of direct instruction? List strategies and examples.

1. State the learning objective and orient students to lesson.
   PURPOSE: inform students of lesson purpose, establish attitude, arouse curiosity
   STRATEGY: state as specific change in behavior, skill level, attitude; pose questions
   EXAMPLE: "After the lesson you will be able to . . ." or "Have you ever wondered why . . . ?"
2. Review the prerequisites.
   PURPOSE: access prior knowledge
   STRATEGY: review material learned previously
   EXAMPLE: "Yesterday we learned . . ."
3. Present new material.
   PURPOSE: present new information or skills
   STRATEGY: organize logically, clearly; explain and demonstrate
   EXAMPLE: "The lesson for today is about . . ."
4. Conduct learning probe.
   PURPOSE: assess students' understanding of new material
   STRATEGY: questioning—written, physical, or oral
   EXAMPLE: "Let's review what has been discussed . . ."
5. Provide independent practice.
   PURPOSE: practice using newly learned concepts
   STRATEGY: seatwork, monitored by teacher
   EXAMPLE: "Work on questions 1 -10 . . ."
6. Assess performance and provide feedback.
   PURPOSE: determine if students have mastered the objective
   STRATEGY: ranges from informal questioning to formal written exam
   EXAMPLE: "You will take a short quiz . . ."
7. Provide distributed practice and review.
   PURPOSE: practice newly learned concepts independently
   STRATEGY: homework
   EXAMPLE: "By tomorrow, complete the following . . . "

2. KEY CONCEPTS, PRINCIPLES, AND THEORIES

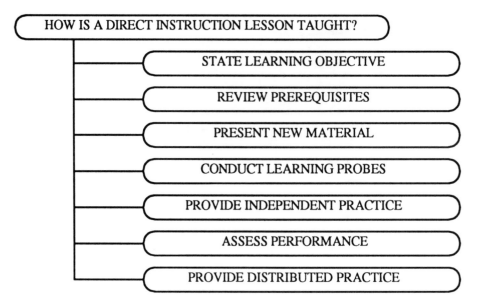

HOW IS A DIRECT INSTRUCTION LESSON TAUGHT?

STATE LEARNING OBJECTIVE

REVIEW PREREQUISITES

PRESENT NEW MATERIAL

CONDUCT LEARNING PROBES

PROVIDE INDEPENDENT PRACTICE

ASSESS PERFORMANCE

PROVIDE DISTRIBUTED PRACTICE

III. WHAT DOES RESEARCH ON DIRECT INSTRUCTION SUGGEST?

1. SELF-CHECK ITEM: List three variants of direct instruction. What does research suggest about the effectiveness of each?

TYPICAL RESPONSE: Describe variants of direct instruction and discuss research findings.

Hunter Mastery Program:	Hunter's program provides a general guide to effective lessons in any subject or grade level. Segments include: 1) getting started; 2) input and modeling; 3) checking for understanding; and 4) independent practice. Research on the effectiveness of the Hunter program is mixed.
Missouri Math Program:	The Missouri math program originates from research conducted on effective teachers and less effective teachers. The principle features include: 1) opening; 2) development; 3) seatwork; 4) homework; and 5) special review. Research shows that the Missouri math program students gained somewhat more in math knowledge than students in a control group.
Systematic Instruction Models:	Systematic instruction models are highly structured, direct instruction programs. Some (e.g., DISTAR) have shown improvements in academic achievement in math for disadvantaged, low achieving students.

2. KEY CONCEPTS, PRINCIPLES, AND THEORIES

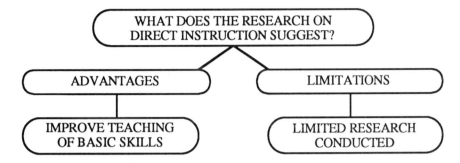

IV. HOW DO STUDENTS LEARN AND TRANSFER CONCEPTS?

1. SELF-CHECK ITEM: Describe how you would use the following approaches to teach your students using a rule-example-rule approach and an examples and non-examples approach.

TYPICAL RESPONSE: Describe rule-example-rule and examples/non-examples teaching approaches.

rule-example-rule approach: state a definition, present several instances of the definition, then restate the definition and show how the instances typify the definition

examples and non-examples: order the examples from easy to difficult, select examples that differ from one another; then, compare examples and non-examples

2. KEY CONCEPTS, PRINCIPLES, AND THEORIES

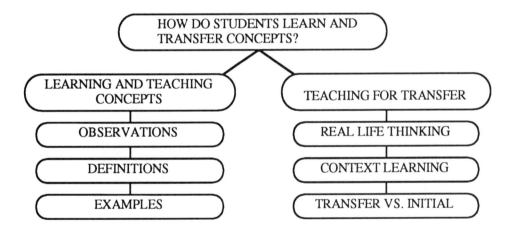

V. HOW ARE DISCUSSIONS USED IN INSTRUCTION?

1. SELF-CHECK ITEM: Create a two-column chart comparing whole-class discussion and small-group discussion. Use the following categories for your chart: appropriate uses, prerequisites, benefits, and limitations.

TYPICAL RESPONSE: Create a chart about whole-class and small-group discussions.

	WHOLE CLASS DISCUSSION	SMALL GROUP DISCUSSION
appropriate uses	inquiry training, exploring points of view	discuss particular topic or parts of topic
prerequisites	adequate knowledge base	lesson presentation
benefits	exploration of diverse views and theories	exploration of diverse views and theories (most effective when controversy is explored) provides for extensive student input
limitations	limited to questions with multiple answers or possibilities	limited to questions with multiple answers or possibilities

2. KEY CONCEPTS, PRINCIPLES, AND THEORIES

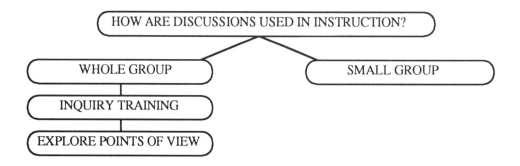

FOR YOUR ENJOYMENT

This section of the study guide includes suggestions for enriching your understanding of a chapter heading you have mastered. You will find information on activities related to the heading and suggestions for research papers, interviews, or presentation.

I. WHAT IS DIRECT INSTRUCTION?

1. In your own classes, identify the elements of direct instruction you observe.

2. Review teacher manuals. Select several examples of direct instruction approaches.

II. HOW IS A DIRECT INSTRUCTION LESSON TAUGHT?

1. Review the variants of direct instruction (e.g., Gagne, Slavin, Hunter). Discuss the advantages and disadvantages of each. Select the one that best fits you.

2. Design a lesson using a direct instruction approach.

III. WHAT DOES RESEARCH ON DIRECT INSTRUCTION SUGGEST?

1. For a research paper, review the literature on the effectiveness of direct instruction.

IV. HOW DO STUDENTS LEARN AND TRANSFER CONCEPTS?

1. For a research paper, review the literature on teaching for transfer.

V. HOW ARE DISCUSSIONS USED IN INSTRUCTION?

1. Make a list of open-ended or controversial discussion questions appropriate for your area of study.

CHAPTER SEVEN: SELF-ASSESSMENT

DIRECTIONS: Below are questions related to the main ideas presented in the chapter. Correct answers or typical responses can be found at the end of the study guide.

1. Which of the following strategies does not belong in a direct instruction lesson?

    A. Provide immediate feedback.
    B. Allow students to control the learning activities.
    C. Set clear and meaningful goals.
    D. Monitor student progress.

2. The seven steps in a direct instruction lesson are listed below in alphabetical order. Rearrange the steps in the proper order.

    A. Assess performance and provide feedback.
    B. Conduct learning probes.
    C. Present new material.
    D. Provide distributed practice and review.
    E. Provide independent practice.
    F. Review prerequisites.
    G. State learning objectives and orient students to lesson.

3. Teacher demonstrations take place during which step of a direct instruction lesson?

    A. Present new material.
    B. Provide independent practice.
    C. Assess performance.
    D. Review prerequisites.

4. List three strategies that make independent practice time effective.

5. Direct instruction methods work best in all of the following contexts except

    A. teaching basic skills.
    B. elementary reading.
    C. teaching low achievers.
    D. teaching critical thinking skills.

6. List several advantages and several limitations of direct instruction.

7. Which of the following conclusions is supported by research?

    A. Give low achievers as much time to respond as high achievers.
    B. Call on another student if a student does not answer quickly.
    C. Call on volunteers rather than selecting students randomly.
    D. Call on a student, then ask a question.

8. Which of the following situations best illustrates transfer of learning?

    A. Students who carefully study do well on a quiz.
    B. Students use their knowledge in one subject to solve problems in another.
    C. Students rehearse after memorizing.
    D. Students correctly identify an example of a concept being taught.

9. All of the following are appropriate for whole-class and small-group discussions except

    A. subjective and controversial issues.
    B. difficult and novel concepts.
    C. affective topics.
    D. questions with simple answers.

10. How would you address the following situations in a whole class discussion?

    A. a student who never makes a comment
    B. a student who talks too much
    C. a student who argues
    D. a student who interrupts

PRACTICE TEST ANSWERS

1. True; Direct instruction involves teacher-directed activities based on specific objectives.

2. False; Direct instruction is appropriate when teaching a well-defined body of information or skills.

3. True; There is agreement among educators as to a specific sequence of events that characterize effective direct instruction lessons.

4. Motivation, apprehending, acquisition, retention, recall, generalization, performance, feedback

5. False; The sequence of activities included in an effective lesson does not vary by grade level.

6. False; The sequence of activities included in an effective lesson does not vary by subject.

7. State learning objective. Orient students to lesson. Review prerequisites. Present new material. Conduct learning probes. Provide independent practice. Assess performance and provide feedback. Provide distributed practice and review.

8. Master teacher models; This category includes Madeline Hunter's mastery teaching and the Missouri math program.

9. Systematic instruction models. These are similar to the mastery teaching models. They are highly structured and inclusive of non-academic events.

10. Anticipatory set; Anticipation is created in students by focusing their attention on the material to be presented, reminding them of what they already know and stimulating their interest in the lesson.

11. B; Despite widespread popularity, evaluations of Hunter's mastery teaching program have not generally found that the students of teachers trained in the model have learned more than other students.

12. C; DISTAR increased the academic achievement levels of disadvantaged low achievers.

13. One advantage of direct instruction is that it can improve the teaching of basic skills. A second advantage is that it is a structured, systematic instructional program.

14. One limitation of direct instruction is that, to date, research has focused on reading and math, but not on other subjects. A second limitation is that it is sometimes uncritically applied to educational settings with the belief that changes will occur. A final limitation is that there is not enough research at the secondary level.

15. True; A concept is a category under which specific elements may be grouped.

16. False; A rule-example-rule approach gives students a definition, then asks students to consider examples and non-examples.

17. True; Transfer of knowledge from one domain to another is dependent upon the similarity between the two.

18. False; It can never be assumed that transfer of learning has occurred.

19. The three rules are: 1) order the examples from easy to difficult; 2) select examples that differ from one another; and 3) compare and contrast examples and non-examples.

20. Teaching for transfer requires the ability to apply knowledge to a variety of circumstances; therefore, similar examples, less similar examples, and non-examples are used to facilitate the process. Initial learning requires that very similar examples be used.

21. Learning objectives that work best for discussion focus on content without simple answers, contain difficult concepts that challenge misconceptions, and are affective in nature.

22. Inquiry training involves presenting students with a puzzling event or experiment that they must solve through theory generation and hypothesis testing.

23. Exploring points of view involves asking students to explore ideas and develop their own beliefs about newly learned information.

24. One teacher function is to guide the discussion. A second function is to help the class avoid dead ends.

25. The teacher prepares the students (with lessons and clear instructions about the group's task). The group leader keeps the group on task and ensures that all group members participate. The group secretary records the group's ideas.

8
STUDENT-CENTERED AND CONSTRUCTIVIST APPROACHES TO INSTRUCTION

CHAPTER OVERVIEW

The purpose of this chapter is to discuss several student-centered and constructivist approaches to instruction. Several main points from the chapter are listed below.

Student-centered and constructivist approaches to instruction include cooperative, discovery, and self-regulated learning.

Student-centered and constructivist approaches to instruction include several cooperative learning approaches such as team assisted individualization, student teams-achievement division, cooperative integrated reading and composition, jigsaw, learning together, and group investigation.

Student-centered and constructivist approaches to instruction emphasize creative problem solving and critical thinking skills.

CHAPTER OUTLINE

I. WHAT IS THE CONSTRUCTIVIST VIEW OF LEARNING?
    A. Historical Roots of Constructivism
    B. Top Down Processing
    C. Cooperative Learning
    D. Discovery Learning
    E. Self-Regulated Learning
    F. Scaffolding
    G. Constructivist Methods in the Content Areas
    H. Research on Constructivist Methods

II. HOW IS COOPERATIVE LEARNING USED IN INSTRUCTION?
    A. Cooperative Learning Methods
    B. Research on Cooperative Learning

III. HOW ARE PROBLEM SOLVING AND THINKING SKILLS TAUGHT?
    A. The Problem Solving Process
    B. Obstacles to Problem Solving
    C. Teaching Creative Problem Solving
    D. Teaching Thinking Skills
    E. Critical Thinking

PRACTICE TEST

DIRECTIONS: Each chapter heading from the text listed below is followed by a series of related questions worth a total of ten points. Respond to each question, check your answers with those found at the end of the study guide chapter, then determine your score. Consider nine points per heading to be mastery.

For those headings on which you do not score at least nine points, turn to the FOR YOUR INFORMATION section of the study guide for corrective instruction. For those headings on which you do score at least nine points, turn to the FOR YOUR ENJOYMENT section of the study guide for enrichment activities.

I. WHAT IS A CONSTRUCTIVIST VIEW OF LEARNING?

True or False

1. (1 point) _____ The main point of constructivist theory is that learners must individually discover and transform complex information if they are to make it their own.

2. (1 point) _____ Constructivist theory draws heavily on the work of Vygotsky and Piaget.

3. (1 point) _____ Constructivists advocate discovery learning.

Multiple Choice

4. (1 point) _____ All of the following explanations address the connection between constructivist approaches and cooperative learning except
   A. the combination emphasizes the social nature of learning.
   B. the combination uses peers to model appropriate ways of thinking.
   C. the combination allows for students' basic knowledge to become complex knowledge.
   D. the combination requires students to challenge their misconceptions.

Short Answer/Essay

5. (2 points) List two arguments in favor of cooperative learning.

_____

_____

6. (4 points) List two advantages of discovery learning and explain why they are advantages.

_____

_____

_____

_____

II. HOW IS COOPERATIVE LEARNING USED IN INSTRUCTION?

True or False

7. (1 point) _____ Cooperative learning refers to instructional methods in which students work together in small groups in order to help each other learn.

8. (1 point) _____ Research indicates that cooperative learning is effective in grades two through twelve in all subjects.

9. (2 points) *Short Answer/Essay*
List the two conditions necessary for student achievement when a cooperative learning approach is used.

_____

_____

10. (6 points) List the characteristics associated with jigsaw, learning together, and group investigation.

_____

_____

_____

III. HOW ARE PROBLEM SOLVING AND THINKING SKILLS TAUGHT?

11. (1 point) _____ *True or False*
Problem solving abilities are innate and, therefore, cannot be taught.

12. (1 point) _____ One indication of transfer of learning is the ability to use information and solve problems.

13. (1 point) _____ *Sentence Completion*
is the term used to describe how individuals fail to see new problem solving alternatives because they are locked into the conventional.

14. (3 points) *Short Answer/Essay*
Briefly describe the following problem solving steps: mean-ends analysis, extracting relevant information, and representing the problem.

_____

_____

_____

15. (4 points) List the steps necessary for creative problem solving.

_____

_____

_____

_____

SCORING	POINTS NEEDED FOR MASTERY	POINTS RECEIVED
I. WHAT IS THE CONSTRUCTIVIST VIEW OF LEARNING?	9	
II. HOW IS COOPERATIVE LEARNING USED IN INSTRUCTION?	9	
III. HOW ARE PROBLEM SOLVING AND THINKING SKILLS TAUGHT?	9	

FOR YOUR INFORMATION

This section of the study guide includes suggestions for further study of the information you have not yet mastered. You will find information on: 1) typical responses to the SELF-CHECK item(s) from the text; and 2) key concepts, principles, and theories addressed in the text chapter.

I. WHAT IS THE CONSTRUCTIVIST VIEW OF LEARNING?

1. SELF-CHECK ITEM: Write a short essay explaining how each of the following terms is related to constructivist theory: (1) cooperative learning; (2) discovery learning; and (3) self-regulated learning.

TYPICAL RESPONSE: Write a short essay using key terms.

A revolution known as "constructivism" is taking place in educational psychology. It builds on Piagetian and Vygotskian concepts of learning—that learners must be active and that learning must involve *discovery* and inquiry and relate to the real world. Constructivist approaches to teaching typically make extensive use of *cooperative learning*, on the theory that students will more easily discover and comprehend difficult concepts if they can talk with each other about the problems. Constructivism creates *self-regulated learning* because students are required to be knowledgeable about effective learning strategies and know when to use them.

2. KEY CONCEPTS, PRINCIPLES, AND THEORIES

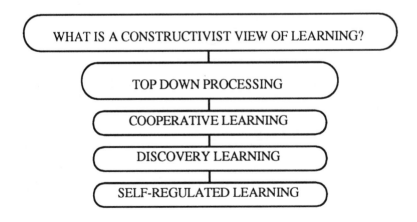

II. HOW IS COOPERATIVE LEARNING USED IN INSTRUCTION?

1. SELF-CHECK ITEM: Explain how each of the following cooperative learning methods can be used in the classroom: (1) Jigsaw; (2) Learning Together; (3) Group Investigation, and (4) Cooperative Scripting.

TYPICAL RESPONSE: Give examples of cooperative learning approaches.

Jigsaw	Students are assigned to six-member teams to work on academic material that has been broken down into sections. For example, a biography might be divided into early life, first accomplishments, major setbacks, later life, and impact on history. Each team member reads his or her section. Next, members of different teams who have studied the same section meet in expert groups to discuss their sections. Then the students return to their teams and take turns teaching their teammates about their section.
Learning Together	Students work in four- or five-member heterogeneous groups on assignments. The groups hand in a single completed assignment and receive praise and reward based on the group product.
Group Investigation	Students work in small groups using cooperative inquiry, group discussion, and cooperative planning and projects. In this method, students form their own two- to six-member groups. After choosing subtopics from a unit that the entire class is studying, the groups break their subtopics into individual tasks and carry out the activities that are necessary to prepare group reports. Each group then makes a presentation or display to communicate findings to the entire class.
Cooperative Scripting	Students work in pairs and take turns summarizing sections of material for one another. While one student summarizes, the other listens and corrects any errors or omissions. Then the two students switch roles, continuing in this way until they have covered all the material to be learned.

2. KEY CONCEPTS, PRINCIPLES, AND THEORIES

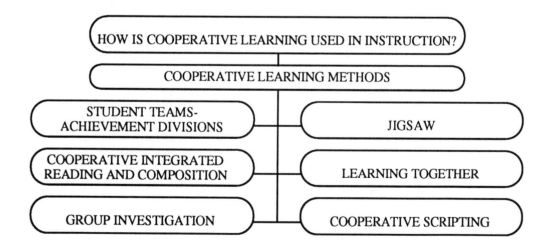

119

III: HOW ARE PROBLEM SOLVING AND THINKING SKILLS TAUGHT?

1. SELF-CHECK ITEM: Describe the problem solving process. Give an example of an obstacle to problem solving.

Students can be taught several well-researched strategies to use in solving problems. The IDEAL method involves:

I	Identify problems and opportunities.
D	Define goals and represent the problem.
E	Explore possible strategies.
A	Anticipate outcomes and act.
L	Look back and learn.

Functional fixedness is a block to the problem solving process caused by an inability to see new uses for familiar objects or ideas. For example, make an "ok" sign by joining the tip of your thumb with the tip of your forefinger. Now, poke your head through the hole made by the "ok" sign. If you think that the hole is not big enough to poke your head through, you do not understand the problem correctly. To solve the problem, you should move your hand making the "ok" sign to your forehead, then take your other forefinger and poke your head through the hole. Thus, your head does not go through the hole; your other forefinger does.

2. KEY CONCEPTS, PRINCIPLES, AND THEORIES

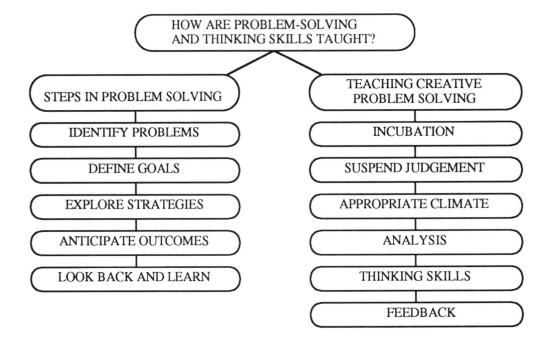

FOR YOUR ENJOYMENT

This section of the study guide includes suggestions for enriching your understanding of a chapter heading you have mastered. You will find information on activities related to the heading and suggestions for research papers, interviews, or presentations.

I. WHAT IS THE CONSTRUCTIVIST VIEW OF LEARNING?

1. For a research paper, review the literature on constructivism.

2. Create lessons using a discovery approach.

II. HOW IS COOPERATIVE LEARNING USED IN INSTRUCTION?

1. For a research paper, review the literature on cooperative learning.

III. HOW ARE PROBLEM SOLVING AND THINKING SKILLS TAUGHT?

1. Design a lesson that enhances problem-solving skills.

2. For a research paper, review the literature on problem solving.

CHAPTER EIGHT: SELF-ASSESSMENT

DIRECTIONS: Below are questions related to the main ideas presented in the chapter. Correct answers or typical responses can be found at the end of the study guide.

1. Constructivism has its roots in the works of

    A. Piaget and Vygotsky.
    B. behaviorists.
    C. moral development theorists.
    D. Albert Bandura.

2. In assisted or mediated learning, the teacher

    A. lets students explore topics to further their learning.
    B. presents information in a structured lesson.
    C. guides instruction so that students acquire learning tools.
    D. gives instruction in basic skills.

3. All of the following strategies reflect a constructivist view of learning except

    A. self-regulated learning.
    B. cooperative learning.
    C. bottom-up processing.
    D. discovery learning.

4. Define scaffolding and give an example of how it is used in the classroom.

5. Research suggests that cooperative learning programs are effective under all of the following conditions except when

    A. the group receives rewards or recognition for achievement.
    B. the groups are mixed in terms of race, ethnicity, gender, and special needs.
    C. the success of the group depends on the individual learning of each group member.
    D. the students are grouped by ability.

6. Match the cooperative learning method with its definition.

_____ Groups work together, then hand in a single completed assignment.

    A. jigsaw

    B. learning together

_____ Groups choose subtopics from a unit that the entire class is studying, then present to others.

    C. group investigation

_____ Groups work on academic material that is broken down into sections.

7. What does the research on cooperative learning say about its effectiveness?

    A. No significant difference is seen between cooperative learning and traditional teaching approaches.
    B. Only the jigsaw method of cooperative learning shows significant differences in achievement over traditional learning methods.
    C. The results of studies consistently show that, with rewards and individual accountability, cooperative learning strategies are superior to traditional teaching methods.

8. Describe an example of discovery learning. What is the teacher's role in a discovery lesson? What strengths and limitations exist with discovery learning?

9. Problem solving may require all of the following skills except

    A. critical thinking.
    B. divergent thinking.
    C. functional fixedness.
    D. brainstorming.

10. How can teachers improve students' problem solving abilities?

PRACTICE TEST ANSWERS

1. True; Constructivists believe learners must transform knowledge in order to make it their own.

2. True; The historical roots of constructivist theory are with Piaget and Vygotsky.

3. True; Constructivists, like Piaget, Vygotsky, and Bruner, advocate discovery learning.

4. C; Constructivist approaches begin with the discovery of basic skills through complex problem solving.

5. Cooperative learning approaches allow students to talk with each other about problems, model appropriate ways of thinking, and expose and challenge each other's misconceptions.

6. Discovery learning arouses students' curiosity, which motivates them to continue working until they find answers. Discovery learning develops problem solving skills and critical thinking because students must analyze and manipulate information.

7. True; Cooperative learning generally refers to groups of four learners who are of mixed abilities.

8. True; Cooperative learning research has found it to be an effective method of instruction.

9. First, there must be some reward or recognition. Second, the success of the group must depend on the individual learning of each group member.

10. Jigsaw groups form teams of experts on a section of the to-be-learned material who teach non-experts. Learning together groups hand in a single completed assignment. Group investigation groups use inquiry, discussion, and cooperative planning and projects.

11. False; Problem solving is a skill that can be taught and learned.

12. True; Transfer of learning requires problem-solving skills.

13. Functional fixedness

14. Means-ends analysis involves deciding what the problem is and what needs to be done. Extracting relevant information means selecting the segments of the problem that contain important information while ignoring other information. Representing the problem accurately is essential in order to solve the problem.

15. The steps necessary for creative problem solving include: incubation, suspension of judgment, establishment of appropriate climate, and analysis.

9
ACCOMMODATING INSTRUCTION TO MEET INDIVIDUAL NEEDS

CHAPTER OVERVIEW

In previous chapters, behavioral and cognitive theories of learning and research on effective instruction were discussed. This chapter shows how instruction is adapted in the classroom to enhance learning. Some of the most effective strategies used to accommodate instruction to individual needs are listed below.

Accommodating instruction to meet individual needs is a product of quality instruction, which is taught at the appropriate level with adequate incentives and time to learn.

Accommodating instruction to meet individual needs includes the use of within-class ability grouping in which students form mixed ability cooperative learning teams that do not segregate lower achievers from their classmates.

Accommodating instruction to meet individual needs includes the use of mastery learning where a pre-established mastery criterion is identified along with opportunities for correction when the criterion is not met and enrichment when it is met.

Accommodating instruction to meet individual needs includes the use of individualized learning strategies—often seen as computer based instruction and cross-age or adult one-on-one tutors—to address learning differences.

CHAPTER OUTLINE

I. WHAT ARE ELEMENTS OF EFFECTIVE INSTRUCTION BEYOND A GOOD LESSON?
    A. Carroll's Model of School Learning and QAIT

II. HOW ARE STUDENTS GROUPED TO ACCOMMODATE ACHIEVEMENT DIFFERENCES?
    A. Between-Class Ability Grouping
    B. Untracking
    C. Regrouping for Reading and Mathematics
    D. Non-graded (Cross-Age Grouping) Elementary Schools
    E. Within-Class Ability Grouping

III. WHAT IS MASTERY LEARNING?
    A. Forms of Mastery Learning
    B. How Mastery Learning Works
    C. Research on Mastery Learning

IV. WHAT ARE SOME WAYS OF INDIVIDUALIZING INSTRUCTION?
   A. Peer Tutoring
   B. Adult Tutoring
   C. Programmed Instruction
   D. Informal Remediation and Enrichment
   E. Computer Based Instruction

V. WHAT EDUCATION PROGRAMS EXIST FOR STUDENTS PLACED AT RISK?
   A. Compensatory Education Programs
   B. Early Intervention Programs

PRACTICE TEST

DIRECTIONS: Each chapter heading from the text listed below is followed by a series of related questions worth a total of ten points. Respond to each question, check your answers with those found at the end of the study guide chapter, then determine your score. Consider nine points per heading to be mastery.

For those headings on which you do not score at least nine points, turn to the FOR YOUR INFORMATION section of the study guide for corrective instruction. For those headings on which you do score at least nine points, turn to the FOR YOUR ENJOYMENT section for enrichment activities.

I. WHAT ARE ELEMENTS OF EFFECTIVE INSTRUCTION BEYOND A GOOD LESSON?

Multiple Choice

1. (1 point) _____ All of the following elements are necessary for effective instruction except

   A. high quality, developmentally appropriate lessons.
   B. adequate incentives for students to learn.
   C. appropriate amounts of time for students to learn.
   D. whole group, teacher-led activities.

2. (1 point) _____ Which statement best depicts Carroll's model of effective instruction?

   A. Learning is the product of aptitude and ability.
   B. Achievement refers to the time needed to learn in relation to the time actually spent learning.
   C. Learning is a measure of the quality of instruction.
   D. A learner's aptitude restricts the amount of information that he or she is capable of learning.

3. (1 point) _____ According to Carroll, which one of the following learning elements is under the direct control of the student?

   A. time to learn
   B. quality of instruction
   C. aptitude to learn
   D. level of instruction

4. (1 point)   _____   A teacher blends strong knowledge of the content with developmentally appropriate teaching strategies, at a developmentally appropriate level, and provides students with adequate practice time for learning. Which part of the QAIT model of effective instruction remains?

A. perseverance
B. quality of instruction
C. incentive
D. opportunity

Matching

5. (4 points)   _____   A teacher creates lessons that match students' prior knowledge and ability.

A. quality of instruction

_____   A teacher gives recognition to students who work diligently to learn the presented material.

B. appropriate level of instruction

_____   A teacher creates lessons that will be interesting, informative, well-organized, and clear to students.

C. incentive

D. time

_____   A teacher recognizes that not all students will complete assignments simultaneously.

Short Answer/Essay

6. (2 points)   Explain the difference between student-controlled elements (from Carroll's model) and teacher-controlled elements (from the QAIT model) that guide effective instruction.

II. HOW ARE STUDENTS GROUPED TO ACCOMMODATE ACHIEVEMENT DIFFERENCES?

Multiple Choice

7. (1 point)   _____   Which example best describes between-class ability grouping?

A. A second grade teacher divides the class into the yellow, blue, and green math groups.
B. Following a math placement test for ninth graders, students with low scores are assigned to remedial math, students with average scores are assigned to pre-algebra, and students with high scores are assigned to algebra I.
C. A teacher's fifth grade class is made up of three cooperative learning groups, each having an equal number of high, mid, and low achievers.
D. Secondary students are allowed to choose courses from a variety of electives and are then assigned to the choices.

8. (1 point) _____ Which example best describes within-class ability grouping?

A. From scores received on an aptitude test, a counselor assigns tenth grade students to either a college preparatory or a general education track.
B. An elementary school groups its students according to their reading level, not their grade level, so that like-ability students are together in a room for reading instruction.
C. Gifted learners from a middle school are brought together for two hours each week for additional science and math instruction.
D. A teacher assigns students to class teams, each consisting of mixed abilities, where students work on reading vocabulary.

9. (1 point) _____ Research shows that all of the following statements are true for between-class ability grouping except

A. between-class ability grouping is more advantageous for low-track class members than for high-track class members.
B. a problem with between-class ability grouping is that placement in a group is often made on the basis of standardized test scores, not course achievement.
C. placing low-achieving students together in one group decreases the possibility that they will be exposed to positive role models.
D. teachers assigned to work with low-track classes exhibit less enthusiasm and organization than teachers assigned to work with high-track classes.

10. (1 points) _____ Which of the following is a true statement regarding effective within-class grouping, according to the research presented in the text?

A. Students of all achievement levels benefit from within-class ability groups.
B. Teachers' expectations of advanced students are lower in homogeneous ability groups than in heterogeneous ability groups.
C. Within-class ability groups have stigmatizing effects on low-achievers.

Short Answer/Essay

11. (6 points) List three types of between-class ability grouping strategies and three types of within-class ability grouping strategies used in reading or mathematics.

_____
_____
_____

III. WHAT IS MASTERY LEARNING?

12. (1 point) _____
True or False
One widely used means of adapting instruction to the needs of diverse students is called mastery learning.

13. (1 point) _____
Multiple Choice
Which statement best describes the basic underlying idea of mastery learning?

A. Making academic comparisons between students foster healthy competition.
B. Grading on the curve is the best approach to assessing student achievement.
C. Whole group instruction that focuses mainly on low achieving students will assure that all students grasp lesson concepts.
D. Students should possess prerequisite skills prior to addressing more advanced skills, regardless of the time it takes to learn the prerequisite skill.

14. (1 point) _____
What is the term used to describe a pre-established standard that a student is required to meet in order to be considered proficient in a skill?

A. mastery criterion
B. remediation
C. enrichment

15. (1 point) _____
An instructional event that helps to broaden the knowledge level of students who have reached mastery level for a given outcome is called

A. an achievement test.
B. a corrective lesson.
C. an enrichment activity.

16. (1 point) _____
What is the term used to describe an instructional event that helps a student to reach mastery level when he or she was unable to do so initially?

A. achievement outcome
B. corrective instruction
C. enrichment activity
D. summative evaluation

17. (1 point) _____ Which of the following statements is a criticism of mastery learning?

A. Mastery learning effects on student achievement are consistently negative.
B. Mastery learning techniques force teachers to become less clear about objectives and how to teach them.
C. Mastery learning involves a trade-off between the amount of content covered and the degree to which students can master each concept.
D. Mastery learning is least effective when used to teach basic skills that form the foundation for later learning.

Short Answer/Essay
18. (4 points) According to Bloom, how is mastery learning different from traditional teaching approaches?

_____
_____
_____
_____

IV. WHAT ARE SOME WAYS OF INDIVIDUALIZING INSTRUCTION?

True or False
19. (1 point) _____ All of the following are examples of individualized instruction except

A. peer tutoring
B. programmed instruction
C. cross-age tutoring
D. norm-referenced evaluation

20. (1 point) _____ According to research cited in the text, which type of tutoring situation is most effective?

A. same-age peer tutoring
B. cross-age, same-ability tutoring
C. same-ability peer tutoring
D. cross-age, cross-ability tutoring

129

21. (1 point) _____ All of the following statements about programmed instruction are true except

A. one advantage of programmed instruction is that large skills are broken down into sub-skills where students proceed step-by-step through a process.
B. one advantage of programmed instruction is that it effectively increases a student's level of achievement across all subject areas.
C. one disadvantage of programmed instruction is that its benefits are often offset by losses in quality of instruction, student motivation, and instructional time.
D. one disadvantage of programmed instruction is that teachers often spend too much time on non-teaching tasks.

22. (1 point) _____ Adult tutoring has all of the following features except that it

A. is one of the most effective instructional strategies known.
B. is expensive.
C. makes use of volunteers.
D. is ineffective with low achievers.

Short Answer/Essay
23. (6 points) Give examples of programmed instruction as it might be used in the classroom.

_____

_____

_____

_____

_____

_____

V. WHAT EDUCATION PROGRAMS EXIST FOR STUDENTS PLACED AT RISK?

True or False
24. (1 point) _____ Compensatory education is designed to prevent or remediate learning problems among students who are from low income families or who attend schools in low income communities.

Short Answer/Essay
25. (2 points) Explain why the term *at risk* was replaced by the term *placed at risk.*

_____

_____

_____

26. (4 points) _____ *Matching*
programs designed to overcome
problems associated with low
socioeconomic status

A. early intervention

B. compensatory

_____ programs that emphasize infant
stimulation, parent training, and
other services from birth to age
five

C. Title 1

D. pull out

_____ programs that are federally funded
for schools to provide extra
educational services

_____ programs in which students are
placed in separate classes for
remediation

Short Answer/Essay

27. (3 points)   Write a brief description of the Reading Recovery program,
early intervention, and Success for All.

_____

_____

_____

SCORING	POINTS NEEDED FOR MASTERY	POINTS RECEIVED
I. WHAT ARE ELEMENTS OF EFFECTIVE INSTRUCTION BEYOND A GOOD LESSON?	9	
II. HOW ARE STUDENTS GROUPED TO ACCOMMODATE ACHIEVEMENT DIFFERENCES?	9	
III. WHAT IS MASTERY LEARNING?	9	
IV. WHAT ARE SOME WAYS OF INDIVIDUALIZING INSTRUCTION?	9	
V. WHAT EDUCATION PROGRAMS EXIST FOR STUDENTS PLACED AT RISK?	9	

FOR YOUR INFORMATION

This section of the study guide includes suggestions for further study of the
information you have not yet mastered. You will find information on: 1) typical responses
to the SELF-CHECK item(s) from the text; and 2) key concepts, principles, and theories
addressed in the text chapter.

I. WHAT ARE ELEMENTS OF EFFECTIVE INSTRUCTION BEYOND A GOOD LESSON?

1. SELF-CHECK ITEM: Draw a diagram showing the significance of and inter-relationship among the following terms: (1) strong incentive; (2) appropriate levels of instruction; (3) high quality of curriculum; (4) high quality of lesson presentation; (5) effective instruction; and (6) optimal use of time.

TYPICAL RESPONSE: Draw a diagram.

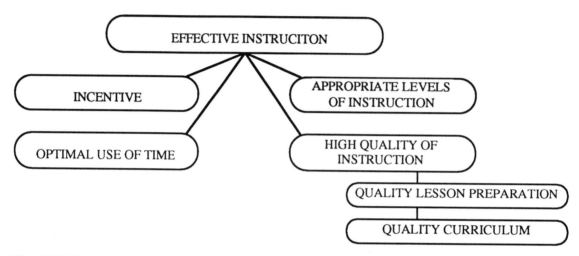

II. HOW ARE STUDENTS GROUPED TO ACCOMMODATE ACHIEVEMENT DIFFERENCES?

1. SELF-CHECK ITEM: Describe the two major types of ability grouping. Give examples of their appropriate use. What does the research literature say about the effectiveness of ability grouping?

TYPICAL RESPONSE: Describe and give examples of two ability groupings.

1. between-class ability grouping: tracking or regrouping into separate classes for particular subjects during part of the school day, such as during pre-algebra or advanced algebra

2. within-class ability grouping: to place students from a mixed-ability class into an appropriate group

TYPICAL RESPONSE: What does the research literature say?

Within-class grouping is more effective than between-class grouping because it provides students with a sense of belonging in the class. Between-class grouping is least beneficial for low-track students because: it is often done on the basis of standardized test scores and not on course content, it exposes students to too few positive role models, and, according to the research, teachers of low-track classes are less enthusiastic, less organized, and teach fewer facts and concepts than do teachers of high-track classes.

3. KEY CONCEPTS, PRINCIPLES, AND THEORIES

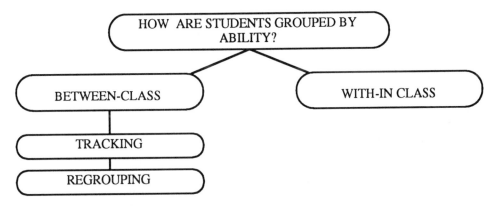

III. WHAT IS MASTERY LEARNING?

1. SELF-CHECK ITEM: Define *mastery learning*. What is its underlying philosophy and assumptions? In what context is mastery learning appropriate? Explain formative assessment, summative assessment, and corrective instruction.

TYPICAL RESPONSE: Explain mastery learning, its philosophy, and the context in which it is used. Explain formative and summative assessment and corrective instruction.

> Mastery learning is a system of instruction that emphasizes the achievement of an instructional objective by allowing time for learning to vary. Mastery learning is based on the idea that all or almost all students should have learned a particular skill to a pre-established mastery criterion prior to moving on to the next skill. Mastery learning is appropriate when additional instructional time is needed for some students.
>
> 1) formative assessment: test of an objective to determine whether or not additional instruction is needed
> 2) summative assessment: final test of an objective
> 3) corrective instruction: additional assignments or activities designed to re-teach concepts to students who do not meet the mastery criterion

2. KEY CONCEPTS, PRINCIPLES, AND THEORIES

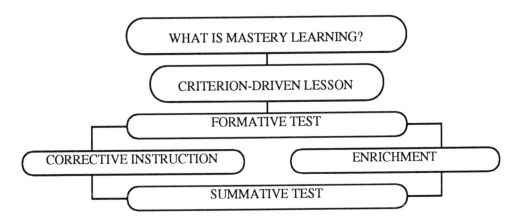

IV. WHAT ARE SOME WAYS OF INDIVIDUALIZING INSTRUCTION?

1. SELF-CHECK ITEM: Describe appropriate ways of individualizing instruction (e.g., peer and adult tutoring, programmed instruction, and computer-based instruction). Explain how drill and practice, tutorials, instructional games, and simulations can be used in classrooms. What does the research literature say about the use of the Internet in classrooms?

TYPICAL RESPONSE: Describe, compare, and identify uses of methods to individualize instruction.

There are several types of tutoring including adult tutoring and peer tutoring. With adult tutoring, one-to-one tutoring is most effective. With peer tutoring, cross-age (where the tutor is older than the tutee) is more effective than same-age peer tutoring.

Programmed instruction materials typically break large skills into smaller skills so that students can work step-by-step. While the idea is feasible, most research has not demonstrated that programmed instruction is effective.

There are several types of computer-assisted instruction. Drill and practice is a widely used, repetitious format where computers provide independent, self-paced practice drills. Tutorials give students self-paced instruction guided by questions. Computer simulation teaches facts, promotes problem solving, and motivates interest by presenting students with realistic models. Educational games are designed to provide students with problem solving abilities, reinforce skills and knowledge, and motivate interest in learning. Utility programs are general purpose programs such as word processing or text editing.

There is little research on the achievement outcomes of Internet involvement, and there is criticism that the Internet is a costly frill that can allow corporate interests to further penetrate schools. There is also serious concerns about students' access to pornography or other inappropriate materials. Yet it seems that the Internet is here to stay.

2. KEY CONCEPTS, PRINCIPLES, AND THEORIES

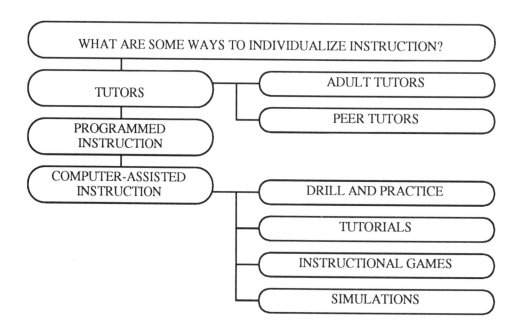

V. WHAT EDUCATION PROGRAMS EXIST FOR STUDENTS PLACED AT RISK?

1. SELF-CHECK ITEM: Define at *risk* and *placed at risk*. What conditions place students at risk? Give examples of compensatory education programs and early intervention programs.

TYPICAL RESPONSE: Define terms, describe conditions, and give examples.

The term "at risk" is borrowed from medicine, in which it has long been used to describe individuals who do not have a given disease but are more likely than average to develop it. Students at risk might come from impoverished or single-parent homes, have marked developmental delays, or exhibit aggressive or withdrawn behaviors. Recently the term "at risk" is often replaced with "placed at risk", which emphasizes the fact that it is often an inadequate response to a learner's needs by school, family, or community that places him or her at risk.

Compensatory education programs are designed to prevent or remediate learning problems for students who are from lower socioeconomic status communities. Compensatory programs include Title 1 and pull-out programs. Early intervention programs target at risk infants and toddlers to prevent possible later need for remediation. They include such programs as Reading Recovery and Success for All.

2. KEY CONCEPTS, PRINCIPLES, AND THEORIES

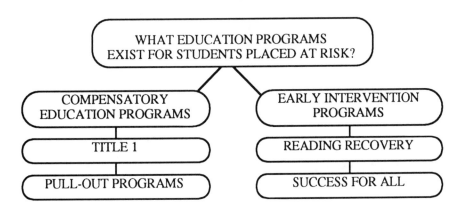

FOR YOUR ENJOYMENT

This section of the study guide includes suggestions for enriching your understanding of a chapter heading you have mastered. You will find information on activities related to the heading and suggestions for research papers, interviews, or presentations.

I. WHAT ARE THE ELEMENTS OF EFFECTIVE INSTRUCTION BEYOND A GOOD LESSON?

1. Observe a classroom teacher and record all the activities that take place in a one hour period, keeping track of the amount of time spent on each activity. Evaluate and report your data in relation to the models of effective teaching presented in this chapter.

2. For a research paper, review the literature on effective teaching.

II. HOW ARE STUDENTS GROUPED TO ACCOMMODATE ACHIEVEMENT DIFFERENCES?

1. Interview a teacher about her or his use of within-class ability grouping. Ask how the groups were formed, what activities the groups encounter, and how the groups are reinforced for appropriate behavior.

2. Describe your ideal teacher for the grade level you plan to teach. Then interview students at that level and ask them to characterize their ideal teacher. How does your description compare with theirs? How do you explain the results?

III. WHAT IS MASTERY LEARNING?

1. Interview a teacher who uses a mastery approach in his or her classroom about its effectiveness.

2. Write objectives, a lesson, and test questions that address one related idea from your discipline.

IV. WHAT ARE SOME WAYS OF INDIVIDUALIZING INSTRUCTION?

1. Select software for instruction in your discipline at the appropriate grade level. Compare the types available for ease of use, type of information given, and assessment qualities.

2. Create a computer drill and practice, simulation, tutorial, or educational game in your discipline that is appropriate for the level of students you intend to teach.

3. For a research paper, review the literature on computer based instruction.

V. WHAT EDUCATION PROGRAMS EXIST FOR STUDENTS PLACED AT RISK?

1. For a research paper, review the literature on students placed at risk.

CHAPTER NINE: SELF-ASSESSMENT

DIRECTIONS: Below are questions related to the main ideas presented in the chapter. Correct answers or typical responses can be found at the end of the study guide.

1. The QAIT model of effective instruction includes which of the following components?

    A. quality of instruction, appropriate levels of instruction, incentive, time
    B. quantity of knowledge, assessment of learning, instructional time, teaching effectiveness
    C. quality of curriculum, affective outcomes, inclusion, tutoring
    D. question, assess, intervene, teach

2. Match the following elements from Carroll's model of instruction with its example.

_____ Students have prerequisite skills.   A. aptitude

_____ The teacher sets aside extra class time.   B. understand instruction

_____ Students are eager to study until the skills are mastered.   C. perseverance

                                              D. quality of instruction

_____ The lesson is presented in such a way that students learn quickly.

3. Which of the following statements represents a basic assumption of mastery learning?

     A. Levels of achievement vary while learning time is constant.
     B. Achievement level and learning time are flexible.
     C. Achievement level and learning time are fixed.
     D. Learning time varies while level of achievement is constant.

4. All of the following are central features of mastery learning except

     A. norm-referenced tests that compare students to each other.
     B. formative quizzes that provide feedback on the student's progress.
     C. summative exams that assess performance at the conclusion of a lesson.
     D. corrective instruction that is given when mastery is not achieved.

5. Placing students in mixed-ability groups and holding them to high standards while providing a variety of instructional approaches is called

     A. compensatory education.
     B. remediation.
     C. individualized instruction.
     D. untracking.

6. Describe the difference between within-class and between-class ability grouping.

7. Which of the following statements about peer tutoring is accurate?

     A. Peer tutoring is an ineffective strategy for teaching secondary-level students.
     B. Peer tutoring increases the achievement of both the tutees and the tutors.
     C. Peer tutoring yields greater achievement gains for tutees than for tutors.
     D. Peer tutoring is an ineffective strategy for teaching elementary-level students.

8. Individualized instruction methods in which students work on self-instructional materials at their own levels and rates is called

     A. early intervention.
     B. programmed instruction.
     C. cooperative learning.
     D. ability grouping.

9. Which of the following statements about the use of the Internet in classrooms is accurate?

A. Most research studies show that the Internet is a powerful and cost-efficient learning tool.
B. The Internet limits students' abilities to communicate with others.
C. There is little research on the achievement outcomes of Internet involvement.
D. Research demonstrates that the Internet decreases a student's achievement level.

10. Educational programs for students who are at risk that prevent or remediate learning problems and target students from poor or disadvantaged backgrounds include all of the following except

A. compensatory education.
B. special education.
C. Title I.
D. intervention programs.

PRACTICE TEST ANSWERS

1. D; Whole group, teacher-led activities are not essential elements of effective instruction.

2. B; Achievement equals time needed in relation to time spent.

3. C; aptitude to learn

4. C; incentive

5. B, C, A, D; Appropriate level of instruction requires consideration of students' needs and abilities. Incentive means to give recognition. Quality of instruction includes planning lessons that are interesting, well-organized, and clear. Time refers to recognizing that students will not all complete assignments simultaneously.

6. Student controlled elements include aptitude, ability to understand instruction, and perseverance. Teacher controlled elements include quality of instruction, appropriate levels of instruction, incentive, and time.

7. B; Using test scores to place students in different classes is an example of between-class ability grouping.

8. D; A within-class ability group would consist of students who are at different levels of ability working together.

9. A; Between-class ability grouping is advantageous for high-track class members.

10. A; Within-class ability groups can benefit all students.

11. Between class ability groups include college preparatory or general track, math placement, or gifted programs. Within-class ability groups include reading groups, math groups, or study groups.

12. True; Mastery learning is used to adapt instruction to individual needs.

13. D; Students should possess prerequisite skills prior to learning new skills.

14. A; mastery criterion

15. C; an enrichment activity

16. B; corrective instruction

17. C; The central problem of mastery learning is that it involves a trade-off between the amount of content that can be covered and the degree to which students master each concept.

18. Bloom proposed that rather than providing all students with the same amount of instructional time and allowing learning to differ, perhaps we should require that all or almost all students reach a certain level of achievement by allowing time to differ.

19. D; norm-referenced evaluations

20. D; cross-age, cross-ability tutoring

21. C; It is not true that programmed instruction benefits are offset by losses in quality of instruction, student motivation, and instructional time.

22. B; The main drawback to adult tutoring is its cost.

23. In one math class, some students might be working on division, others on fraction, others on decimals, and still others on measurement or geometry, all at the same time.

24. True. Compensatory education programs are for students placed at risk.

25. The term *placed at risk* has replaced the term *at risk* because it emphasizes the fact that it is often an inadequate response to a student's needs by school, family, or community.

26. B, A, C, D; Early intervention programs target infants and toddlers. Compensatory education programs prevent or remediate learning problems for students who are from lower socioeconomic status communities. Chapter 1 programs are federally funded and target low income and disadvantaged students. Pull-out programs place students in separate classes for remediation.

27. Early intervention programs target at risk infants and toddlers to prevent the possible later need for remediation. Reading Recovery programs provide one-to-one tutoring from specially trained teachers to first graders who are not reading adequately. Success for All programs provide one-to-one tutoring, family support services, and changes in instruction that might prevent students from falling behind.

10
MOTIVATING STUDENTS TO LEARN

CHAPTER OVERVIEW

The material covered in this chapter focuses on motivation—the internal processes that activate, guide, and maintain behavior. Some of the theoretical concepts associated with motivation are listed below.

Motivation, depending on the theory, can be a consequence of reinforcement, a measure of human need, an attribution of successes and failures, or an expectancy of the probability of success.

Motivation can be enhanced by emphasizing learning goals and empowering attributions.

Motivation to learn can increase when teachers arouse students' interest, maintain their curiosity, use a variety of teaching strategies, state clear expectations, and give frequent and immediate feedback.

Motivation to learn can increase when rewards are contingent, specific, and credible.

CHAPTER OUTLINE

I. WHAT IS MOTIVATION?

II. WHAT ARE SOME THEORIES OF MOTIVATION?
    A. Motivation and Behavioral Learning Theory
    B. Motivation and Human Needs
    C. Motivation and Attribution Theory
    D. Motivation and Expectancy Theory

III. HOW CAN ACHIEVEMENT MOTIVATION BE ENHANCED?
    A. Motivation and Goal Orientations
    B. Learned Helplessness and Attribution Training
    C. Teacher Expectations and Achievement
    D. Anxiety and Achievement

IV. HOW CAN TEACHERS INCREASE STUDENTS' MOTIVATION TO LEARN?
    A. Intrinsic and Extrinsic Motivation
    B. How Can Teachers Enhance Intrinsic Motivation?
    C. Principles for Providing Incentives to Learn

V. HOW CAN TEACHERS REWARD PERFORMANCE, EFFORT, AND IMPROVEMENT?
    A. Using Praise Effectively

B. Teaching Students to Praise Themselves
C. Using Grades as Incentives
D. Individual Learning Expectations
E. Incentive Systems Based on Goal Structure

PRACTICE TEST

DIRECTIONS: Each chapter heading from the text listed below is followed by a series of related questions worth a total of ten points. Respond to each question, check your answers with those found at the end of the chapter, then determine your score. Consider nine points per heading to be mastery.

For those headings on which you do not score at least nine points, turn to the FOR YOUR INFORMATION section of the study guide for corrective instruction. For those headings on which you do score at least nine points, turn to the FOR YOUR ENJOYMENT section of the study guide for enrichment activities.

I. WHAT IS MOTIVATION?

1. (1 point) _____

True or False
Motivation is one of the most important ingredients of effective instruction.

2. (5 points)

Short Answer/Essay
List five factors that can play a role in making students want to learn.

_____

_____

_____

_____

_____

3. (2 points)

Explain how motivation can vary in intensity and direction.

_____

_____

4. (2 points)

Give an example of an activity that promotes intrinsic motivation and an activity that promotes extrinsic motivation.

_____

_____

II. WHAT ARE SOME THEORIES OF MOTIVATION?

5. (1 point) _____

True or False
For behavioral theorists, motivation is a product of reinforcement.

6. (1 point) _____ According to Maslow's hierarchy of needs, growth needs must be met before deficiency needs.

7. (1 point) _____ According to human needs theory, self-actualization is the desire to become everything that one is capable of becoming.

Short Answer/Essay

8. (4 points) Attribution theory deals primarily with four explanations for success or failure in achievement situations. List them.

_____
_____
_____
_____

9. (1 point) According to expectancy theory, motivation is based on what formula?

_____

10. (2 points) Explain the implications for expectancy theory in the classroom.

_____
_____

III. HOW CAN ACHIEVEMENT MOTIVATION BE ENHANCED?

Multiple Choice

11. (1 point) _____ Which of the following statements best defines achievement motivation?

A. an explanation of motivation that focuses on how people explain the causes for their own successes and failures
B. the generalized tendency to strive for success and to choose goal-oriented success/failure activities
C. motivation created by external factors like rewards and punishments
D. behavior that is directed toward satisfying personal standards of behavior

12. (1 point) _____ Students who take difficult courses and seek challenges are motivationally oriented toward what type of goals?

A. expectancy goals
B. outcome goals
C. performance goals
D. learning goals

13. (1 point) _____

Sentence Completion
are individuals who are motivated to achieve, according to Atkinson.

14. (1 point _____

is an extreme form of the motive to avoid failure.

15. (2 points)

Short Answer/Essay
List two ways in which teachers can make testing situations less stressful.

_____

_____

16. (4 points)

List the four general principles associated with helping students who have shown a tendency to accept failure.

_____

_____

_____

_____

IV. HOW CAN TEACHERS INCREASE STUDENTS' MOTIVATION TO LEARN?

17. (1point) _____

Sentence Completion
is a type of motivation associated with activities that serve as their own reward

18. (1 point) _____

is a type of motivation associated with activities that require reinforcers.

19. (4 points)

Short Answer/Essay
List four strategies teachers can use to promote intrinsic motivation.

_____

_____

_____

_____

20. (4 points)

List four strategies teachers can use to promote extrinsic motivation.

_____

_____

_____

_____

V. HOW CAN TEACHERS REWARD PERFORMANCE, EFFORT, AND IMPROVEMENT?

21. (1 point) _____

True or False
Incentive strategies used in the classroom should focus on student ability.

22. (2 points)

Short Answer/Essay
List two ways to reward students' performance.

_____

_____

23. (3 points)   List three characteristics of effective praise.

_____

_____

_____

24. (3 points)   List three functions for grades.

_____

_____

_____

25. (1 point)   Define "goal structure."

_____

SCORING	POINTS NEEDED FOR MASTERY	POINTS RECEIVED
I. WHAT IS MOTIVATION?	9	
II. WHAT ARE SOME THEORIES OF MOTIVATION?	9	
III. HOW CAN ACHIEVEMENT MOTIVATION BE ENHANCED?	9	
IV. HOW CAN TEACHERS INCREASE STUDENTS' MOTIVATION TO LEARN?	9	
V. HOW CAN TEACHERS REWARD PERFORMANCE, EFFORT, AND IMPROVEMENT?	9	

FOR YOUR INFORMATION

This section of the study guide includes suggestions for further study of the information you have not yet mastered. You will find information on: 1) typical responses to the SELF-CHECK item(s) from the text; and 2) key concepts, principles, and theories addressed in the text chapter.

I. WHAT IS MOTIVATION?

1. SELF-CHECK ITEM: Explain how motivation has intensity and direction.

TYPICAL RESPONSE: Explain motivation.

> Motivation is an internal process that activates, guides, and maintains behavior over time. Individuals
> are motivated for different reasons, with different intensities, and in different directions. For example,
> a student may be highly motivated to study for a social studies test in order to get a high grade (extrinsic
> motivation) and highly motivated to study for a math test because he or she is interested in the subject
> (intrinsic motivation).

2. KEY CONCEPTS, PRINCIPLES, AND THEORIES.

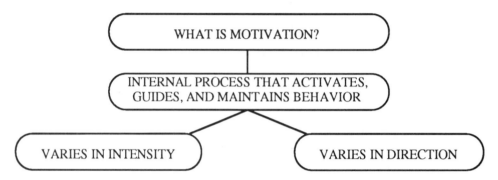

II. WHAT ARE SOME THEORIES OF MOTIVATION?

1. SELF-CHECK ITEM: Organize the information from this section into a chart that
includes the following headings: Behavioral Learning Theory, Human Needs Theory,
Attribution Theory, and Expectancy Theory. For each one, define the underlying concept;
identify any key experiments; and briefly describe and illustrate how the model works.
Identify applications and implications for classroom teachers of each of the theories.

TYPICAL RESPONSE: Organize information into schema.

THEORIES	CONCEPT	EXPERIMENT/ THEORIST	WORKINGS OF MODEL	EDUCATIONAL APPLICATIONS
BEHAVIORAL	motivation is product of reinforcement	Skinner	motivation is determined by personal/situational factors	limited utility
HUMAN NEEDS	motivation is way to satisfy needs	Maslow	deficiency needs must be satisfied before growth needs	meet basic first
ATTRIBUTION	motivation is attributed to internal and external factors	Weiner	attribute success or failure to ability, effort, task difficulty, or luck	feedback influences students' perception of control

| EXPECTANCY | M = Ps X Is | | Atkinson | maintain moderate levels of probability for success | tasks should be neither too easy nor too difficult |

2. KEY CONCEPTS, PRINCIPLES, AND THEORIES

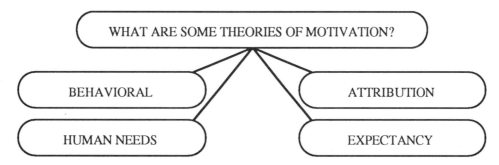

III. HOW CAN ACHIEVEMENT MOTIVATION BE ENHANCED?

1. SELF-CHECK ITEM: Define *achievement motivation.* How do students differ in their approaches to academic success or failure? How can attribution training and changes in teacher expectations affect students' motivation and performance?

TYPICAL RESPONSE: Define and discuss achievement motivation.

> Achievement motivation can be defined as the generalized tendency to strive for success and to choose goal-oriented success/failure activities. Students can be motivationally oriented toward learning (mastery) goals or oriented toward performance goals. Students striving toward learning goals view the purpose of schooling to be gaining competence. They take challenging courses. Students striving toward performance goals seek to gain positive judgments of their competence. They seek good grades by avoiding challenging courses. Teachers can help students by communicating that success is possible. They can wait for students to respond to questions and can avoid unnecessary achievement distinctions among students.

2. KEY CONCEPTS, PRINCIPLES, AND THEORIES

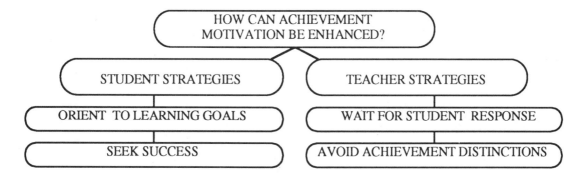

IV. HOW CAN TEACHERS INCREASE STUDENTS' MOTIVATION TO LEARN?

1. SELF-CHECK ITEM: Make a list of intrinsic and extrinsic motivators as well as specific strategies that teachers can use to enhance motivation in their classrooms. Then reread the chapter-opening vignette. Identify each event in Mr. Lewis's lesson in terms of the strategies you have listed.

TYPICAL RESPONSE: Make a list of intrinsic and extrinsic motivators and strategies.

	INTRINSIC	EXTRINSIC
MOTIVATORS	content or material itself serves as motivator	praise, grades, recognition, prizes, special privileges
TEACHER STRATEGIES	arouse interest, maintain curiosity, use a variety of presentation modes	express clear expectations, provide clear, immediate, and frequent feedback
MR. LEWIS' CLASS	aroused interest and curiosity by his attire, role play activity, and presentation style	gave clear directions (secret instructions), provided feedback through formal evaluations on effectiveness of students' presentations, had students work in cooperative groups

2. KEY CONCEPTS, PRINCIPLES, AND THEORIES

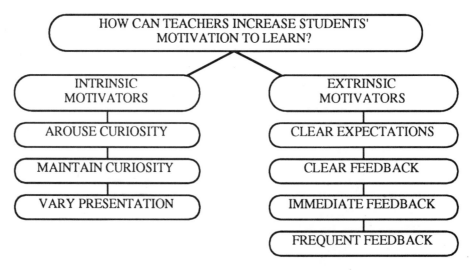

V. HOW CAN TEACHERS REWARD PERFORMANCE, EFFORT, AND IMPROVEMENT?

1. SELF-CHECK ITEM: Explain how rewards, praise, grades, ILE scores, individualized goal structures, and cooperative goal structures can be used appropriately as incentives to enhance students' motivation to learn.

TYPICAL RESPONSE: Explain how incentives can enhance motivation.

rewards: should be for effort rather than ability

148

praise:	praise frequently, making sure it is contingent, specific, and credible
grades:	serve three functions: evaluation, feedback, and incentive
ILE scores:	recognize improvement until students are performing at their peak level
individualized goal structure:	one student's success necessitates another's failure
cooperative goal structure:	recognize efforts of groups so that one student's success facilitates another's success

2. KEY CONCEPTS, PRINCIPLES, AND THEORIES

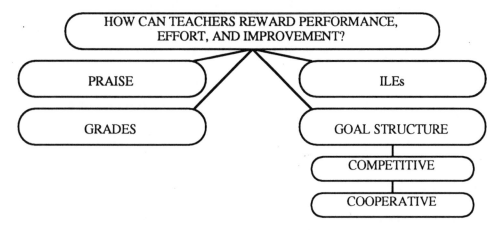

FOR YOUR ENJOYMENT

This section of the study guide includes suggestions for enriching your understanding of a chapter heading you have mastered. You will find information on activities related to the heading and suggestions for research papers, interviews, or presentations.

I. WHAT IS MOTIVATION?

1. Make a list of activities that motivate you, your classmates, and students who you will teach.

II. WHAT ARE SOME THEORIES OF MOTIVATION?

1. For a research paper, review the literature on theories of motivation.

III. HOW CAN ACHIEVEMENT MOTIVATION BE ENHANCED?

1. Interview students about test anxiety. To what do they attribute their anxiety? Analyze their responses in relationship to attribution theory.

2. For a research paper, review the literature on learned helplessness and test anxiety.

IV. HOW CAN TEACHERS INCREASE STUDENTS' MOTIVATION TO LEARN?

1. Create a lesson that includes strategies for increasing students' motivation.

2. Observe in a classroom for one or two hours. Make a list of intrinsic and extrinsic motivational strategies used by the teacher.

V. HOW CAN TEACHERS REWARD PERFORMANCE, EFFORT, AND IMPROVEMENT?

1. Identify rewards you will use in your classroom to improve performance and effort.

CHAPTER TEN: SELF-ASSESSMENT

DIRECTIONS: Below are questions related to the main ideas presented in the chapter. Correct answers or typical responses can be found at the end of the study guide.

1. Rearrange the following needs from Maslow's hierarchy in the proper order.

    A. aesthetic
    B. belongingness and love
    C. need to know and understand
    D. physiological
    E. safety
    F. self-actualization
    G. self-esteem

2. Match each theory of motivation with its definition.

_____ A theory of motivation is closely tied to the principle that behaviors that have been reinforced are likely to be repeated.

_____ An explanation of motivation that focuses on how people explain the causes of their own successes and failures.

_____ A theory that motivation is determined by the probability and incentive value of success.

A. expectancy theory

B. behavioral theory

C. attribution

3. How would Skinner's explanation of a student's incentive to obtain good grades differ from Maslow's explanation?

4. A student with an internal locus of control is likely to attribute a high test grade to

    A. the test being easy.
    B. favored treatment from the teacher.
    C. careful studying.
    D. good luck.

5. Teachers who want their students to work harder regardless of ability level or task difficulty are trying to develop attributions that fall into which of the following categories?

    A. internal-stable
    B. internal-unstable
    C. external-stable
    D. external-unstable

6. A student who tends to choose either very easy or very hard tasks would most likely be

    A. seeking success.
    B. avoiding failure.
    C. risking learned helplessness.
    D. choosing an internal locus of control.

7. Which behavior is characteristic of students who are oriented toward learning goals?

    A. taking a challenging course
    B. trying to make the honor roll
    C. trying to get recognition from the teacher
    D. becoming discouraged in the face of obstacles

8. The main idea underlying the Individual Learning Expectations (ILE) model is

    A. a pass or fail system.
    B. an ungraded evaluation.
    C. grading on the basis of improvement.
    D. criterion-referenced grading.

9. Match the following goal structures with the correct description of each.

_____ All succeed or all fail.   A. competitive

_____ One person's success or failure has no   B. cooperative
        influence on another's fate.
                                                          C. individualized
_____ Some will succeed and others will fail.

10. What are some advantages and disadvantages of being graded on improvement?

PRACTICE TEST ANSWERS

1. True; Motivation is one of the most important components of learning.

2. Students' personality, students' abilities, characteristics of the learning task, incentives for learning, setting teacher behavior

3. Motivation varies in intensity: one student may be more interested in a learning task than another student. Motivation varies in direction: two students can be equally motivated; however, at different tasks.

4. Making a lesson fun, active, and engaging promotes intrinsic motivation. Grades and other rewards, like praise or tokens, promote extrinsic motivation.

5. True; Behavioral theorists argue that there is no need to separate theories of learning from theories of motivation since both are products of reinforcement.

6. False; Deficiency needs are those that are critical to physical and psychological well-being. Growth needs are those that promote understanding, beauty, and relationships.

7. True; Self-actualization is characterized by acceptance of the self and others.

8. Ability, effort, task difficulty, luck

9. motivation = perceived possibility of success times incentive value of success

10. Tasks for students should be neither too difficult nor too easy.

11. B; Achievement motivation is the general desire to be successful and goal-oriented.

12. D; Learning goals-oriented students see the purpose of schooling as gaining competence.

13. Success seekers

14. Learned helplessness

15. Avoid time pressures, begin the test with easy problems, use a simple test format.

16. Accentuate the positive, eliminate the negative, go from familiar to the new, create appropriate problem solving challenges.

17. Intrinsic motivation

18. Extrinsic motivation

19. Arouse interest, maintain curiosity, use a variety of presentation modes, guide learning.

20. Express clear expectations, provide clear feedback, provide immediate feedback, provide frequent feedback.

21. False; Incentive strategies should focus on effort rather than ability.

22. Rewarding directly through praise or indirectly through grades

23. Praise must be contingent upon the task, specific as to what is good, and credible.

24. Evaluation, feedback, incentives

25. Goal structure refers to the degree to which students are in cooperation or competition with one another.

11
EFFECTIVE LEARNING ENVIRONMENTS

CHAPTER OVERVIEW

The focus of this chapter is on prevention of discipline problems as the most effective means of classroom management. Preventing disruptive behaviors increases instructional time, improves teaching effectiveness, and increases on-task student behaviors. Some of the effective prevention strategies are listed below.

Classroom management strategies that impact the amount of time used for learning include avoiding late starts and early finishes, avoiding interruptions, handling routine procedures smoothly and quickly, anticipating needs, and minimizing time spent on discipline.

Classroom management practices that contribute to effective classroom routines start on the first day of school. Developing class rules and procedures that are presented and applied at the beginning of the school year are important prevention strategies.

Classroom management strategies that advocate the "principle of least intervention" are most effective.

Classroom management strategies that apply behavioral analysis are effective in addressing more serious student misbehaviors.

Classroom management procedures that deal with serious student misbehaviors vary; however, those instructors who are effective managers clearly express and consistently enforce their classroom rules in a manner that students believe is fair.

CHAPTER OUTLINE

I. WHAT IS AN EFFECTIVE LEARNING ENVIRONMENT?

II. WHAT IS THE IMPACT OF TIME ON LEARNING?
    A. Using Allocated Time for Instruction
    B. Using Engaged Time Effectively
    C. Can Time on Task Be too High?
    D. Classroom Management in the Student Centered Classroom

III. WHAT PRACTICES CONTRIBUTE TO EFFECTIVE CLASSROOM MANAGEMENT?
    A. Starting Out the Year Right
    B. Setting Class Rules

IV. WHAT ARE SOME STRATEGIES FOR MANAGING ROUTINE MISBEHAVIOR?
    A. Principle of Least Intervention

B. Prevention
C. Nonverbal Cues
D. Praising Behavior That Is Incompatible with Misbehavior
E. Praising Other Students
F. Verbal Reprimands
G. Repeated Reminders
H. Applying Consequences

V. HOW IS APPLIED BEHAVIOR ANALYSIS USED?
A. How Student Misbehavior Is Maintained
B. Principles of Applied Behavior Analysis
C. Applied Behavior Analysis Programs
D. Ethics of Behavioral Models

VI. HOW CAN SERIOUS DISCIPLINE PROBLEMS BE PREVENTED?
A. Causes of Misbehavior
B. Enforcing Rules and Practices
C. Enforcing School Attendance
D. Avoid Tracking
E. Practicing Intervention
F. Requesting Family Involvement
G. Using Peer Mediation
H. Judiciously Applying Consequences

PRACTICE TEST

DIRECTIONS: Each chapter heading listed below is followed by a series of related questions worth a total of ten points. Respond to each question, check your answers with those found at the end of the chapter, then determine your score. Consider nine points per heading to be mastery.

For those headings on which you do not score at least nine points, turn to the FOR YOUR INFORMATION section for corrective instruction. For those headings on which you do score at least nine points, turn to the FOR YOUR ENJOYMENT section for enrichment activities.

I. WHAT IS AN EFFECTIVE LEARNING ENVIRONMENT?

Short Answer/Essay
1. (10 points)   Create a list of classroom management strategies that provide an effective learning environment.

_____
_____
_____
_____
_____

II. WHAT IS THE IMPACT OF TIME ON LEARNING?

2. (1 point) _____

True or False

Two sources of "lost time" are standardized testing and school assemblies.

3. (1 point) _____

One way to avoid late starts and early finishes is to plan more instruction than you think you will need.

4. (1 point) _____

Minor interruptions do little to change the momentum of a lesson.

5. (4 points)

Short Answer/Essay

List four ways in which teachers can use engaged time effectively.

_____

_____

_____

_____

6. (1 point)

Define "withitness."

_____

7. (1 point)

Define "overlapping."

_____

8. (1 point)

Explain how teachers can avoid "mock participation."

_____

III. WHAT PRACTICES CONTRIBUTE TO EFFECTIVE CLASSROOM MANAGEMENT?

9. (1 point) _____

True or False

Elementary teachers need to be concerned with socializing students to the norms and behaviors accepted in school.

10. (1 point) _____

Middle and secondary teachers need to be concerned with motivating students toward self-regulated behaviors.

11. (1 point) _____

Research indicates that the first days of school are critical in establishing classroom order.

12. (3 points)

Short Answer/Essay

List the three principles for setting classroom rules.

_____

_____

_____

13. (4 points)   Identify the four principles of room arrangement for minimizing disruptions.

_____
_____
_____

IV. WHAT ARE SOME STRATEGIES FOR MANAGING ROUTINE MISBEHAVIORS?

True or False

14. (1 point) _____ Teacher behaviors associated with low time on-task were also associated with fewer serious behavior problems.

15. (1 point) _____ The majority of behavior problems a teacher addresses are relatively minor.

Sentence Completion

16. (1 point) _____ is the term used to explain that misbehaviors should be corrected using the simplest strategy that will work.

Short Answer/Essay

17. (7 points)   List, in order from least disruptive to most disruptive, the strategies used to deal with misbehaviors.

_____
_____
_____
_____
_____
_____
_____

V. HOW IS APPLIED BEHAVIOR ANALYSIS USED TO MANAGE MORE SERIOUS BEHAVIOR PROBLEMS?

Multiple Choice

18. (1 point) _____ All of the following are ways in which student misbehavior is maintained except

A. teacher's attention.
B. students' attention.
C. release from boredom.
D. group contingencies.

Order in Sequence

19. (6 points) _____ When the program is working, reduce the reinforcement.
_____ If necessary, choose a punisher and criteria for punishment.
_____ Establish a baseline for the target behavior.
_____ Choose a reinforcer and criteria for reinforcement.
_____ Observe behavior during program implementation and compare it to baseline.
_____ Identify the target behavior(s) and reinforcer(s).

20. (3 points) _____ *Matching*
program in which a student is rated
on behaviors by one or several
teachers; then, if behavior is
appropriate for a specified amount
of time, he or she receives a special
privilege or reward from parents

_____ program in which points or some
other form of rewards are given (to
be exchanged for something desired)
when appropriate behavior is exhibited

_____ program in which an entire group is
rewarded on the basis of the behavior
of the group members

A. daily report
card

B. token
reinforcement

C. group
contingency

VI. HOW CAN SERIOUS BEHAVIOR PROBLEMS BE PREVENTED?

True or False

21. (1 point) _____ From three to eight times as many boys as girls are
estimated to have serious behavior problems.

22. (1 point) _____ Some students misbehave because they perceive that the
rewards for misbehavior outweigh the rewards for a
appropriate behavior.

23. (1 point) _____ Consistently expressing the expectation that students
conform leads to misbehavior.

Short Answer/Essay

24. (7 points) List seven ways in which serious discipline problems can
be prevented.

_____
_____
_____
_____
_____
_____
_____
_____

SCORING	POINTS NEEDED FOR MASTERY	POINTS RECEIVED
I. WHAT IS AN EFFECTIVE LEARNING ENVIRONMENT?	9	
II. WHAT IS THE IMPACT OF TIME ON LEARNING?	9	

III. WHAT PRACTICES CONTRIBUTE TO EFFECTIVE CLASSROOM MANAGEMENT?	9	
IV. WHAT ARE SOME STRATEGIES FOR MANAGING ROUTINE MISBEHAVIOR?	9	
V. HOW IS APPLIED BEHAVIOR ANALYSIS USED TO MANAGE SERIOUS BEHAVIOR PROBLEMS?	9	
VI. HOW CAN SERIOUS BEHAVIOR PROBLEMS BE PREVENTED?	9	

FOR YOUR INFORMATION

This section of the study guide includes suggestions for further study of the information you have not yet mastered. You will find information on: 1) typical responses to the SELF-CHECK item(s) from the text; and 2) key concepts, principles, and theories addressed in the text chapter.

I. WHAT IS AN EFFECTIVE LEARNING ENVIRONMENT?

1. SELF-CHECK ITEM: What elements contribute to an effective learning environment? Make a list of discipline problems that you might encounter as a teacher. How might these problems be prevented or handled?

TYPICAL RESPONSE: What elements contribute to an effective classroom learning environment?

Elements include preventing and responding to misbehavior, using class time well, creating an atmosphere that is conducive to interest and inquiry, and permitting the use of activities that engage students' minds and imaginations.

TYPICAL RESPONSE: Make a list of discipline problems that you might encounter. How do you prevent misbehavior?

What is considered a discipline problem may differ from teacher to teacher. However, inappropriate communications, disrespect, and off-task behaviors generally affect the learning environment. Teachers who present interesting, well-organized lessons, who use incentives for learning effectively, who accommodate their instruction to students' level of preparation, and who plan and manage their own time effectively will have few discipline problems to address.

II. WHAT IS THE IMPACT OF TIME ON LEARNING?

1. SELF-CHECK ITEM: Review the vignette at the beginning of the chapter. Identify all the ways in which time was used in Ms. Cavalho's class, including allocated time and engaged time. List ways in which allocated time and engaged time can be maximized. Give specific examples to show how a teacher might exhibit withitness and overlapping.

TYPICAL RESPONSE: Discuss various ways time impacts learning.

Ms. Cavalho lost time in her classroom when transitions from activity to activity were rough, as with the ability group reading. Students were asked to return to their desks for materials after they were settled and ready to start the activity; thus, a "late start." Ms. Cavalho failed to avoid interruptions when considerable time was spent discussing the cough/sneeze issue.

Allocated time refers to the time during which students have the opportunity to learn. Engaged time is the part of allocated time when students are actually exhibiting on-task behaviors.

There are five ways that allocated time can be maximized. They include: 1) avoiding lost time; 2) avoiding late starts and early finishes; 3) avoiding interruptions; 4) handling routine procedures smoothly and quickly; and 5) minimizing time spent on discipline.

There are six strategies for increasing students' time on-task. They include: 1) teaching engaging lessons;
2) maintaining momentum; 3) maintaining smoothness of instruction; 4) managing transitions;
5) maintaining group focus during lessons; and 6) maintaining group focus during seatwork.

In order to exhibit withitness, teachers need "eyes in the back of their heads." This means that they are aware of what their students are doing at all times. For example, a withit teacher leans over an individual student's desk to help him or her, and, at the same time, knows that the rest of the class is busy. Overlapping refers to a teacher's ability to be actively engaged in more than one activity at a time. For example, a teacher who is presenting a lecture can, without pause, walk over to two students who are off-task and gain their attention.

2. KEY CONCEPTS, PRINCIPLES, AND THEORIES

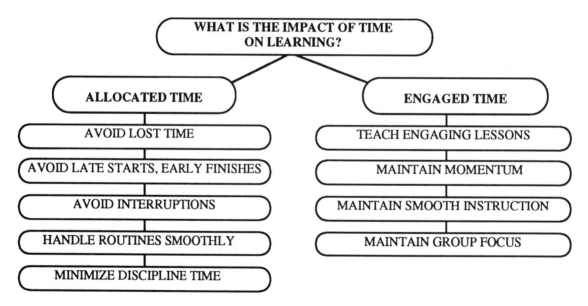

III. WHAT PRACTICES CONTRIBUTE TO EFFECTIVE CLASSROOM MANAGEMENT?

1. SELF-CHECK ITEM: For the grade level you plan to teach, construct a classroom layout and a "To Do" list for starting the academic year in a way that will minimize behavior problems.

TYPICAL RESPONSE: Construct a classroom and a "to do" list.

To Do
* keep high-traffic areas free of congestion
* make all students visible to the teacher
* keep frequently used materials and supplies accessible
* arrange room so all students can see presentation

Rules
* be courteous
* respect property
* be on-task

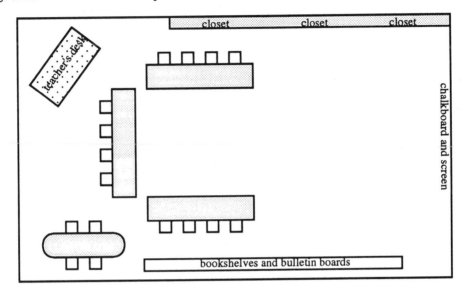

2. KEY CONCEPTS, PRINCIPLES, AND THEORIES

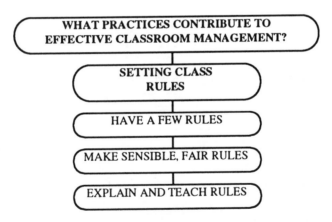

IV. WHAT ARE SOME STRATEGIES FOR MANAGING ROUTINE MISBEHAVIORS?

1. SELF-CHECK ITEM: List the sequence of strategies that are used for managing routine misbehavior according to the principle of least intervention. In each case, how does the strategy work? How would you identify examples of these strategies in student-teacher dialogues? Reread the vignette at the beginning of this chapter. How did Ms. Cavalho manage her students' misbehavior?

TYPICAL RESPONSE: Discuss the principles of least intervention.

SEQUENCE	HOW STRATEGY WORKS
prevention	present interesting lessons, make class rules clear and consistent, keep students busy
nonverbal cues	make eye contact, move closer to misbehaving students, light touch on shoulder
praise good behavior	praise students when they are exhibiting appropriate behaviors
praise other students	praise students who are exhibiting appropriate behaviors as a cue to those who are misbehaving
verbal reminder	soft, simple, immediate verbal reprimand
repeated reminder	includes statement of what is expected, given until student complies
applying consequences	examples include sending students out of class, making students stay after school, removing privileges, and calling students' parents

Ms. Cavalho could have prevented many of her problems by being prepared. Students, prior to moving to another area of the classroom, should have been told exactly what they needed to take with them. This would have eliminated the trips back to their desks for materials. A nonverbal cue to the girl who sneezed (e.g., making eye contact and then directing her by pointing to the tissue on the desk) would have solved this problem.

2. KEY CONCEPTS, PRINCIPLES, AND THEORIES

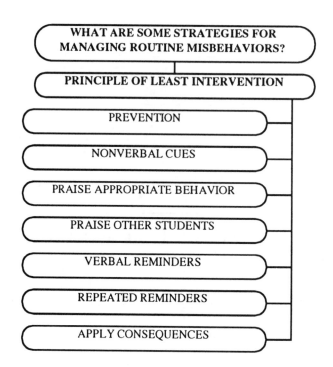

162

V. HOW IS APPLIED BEHAVIOR ANALYSIS USED TO MANAGE MORE SERIOUS BEHAVIOR PROBLEMS?

1. SELF-CHECK ITEM: Explain how applied behavior analysis is used in the classroom. Describe the appropriate and ethical use of praise, home-based reinforcement, punishment, daily report cards, and group contingencies.

TYPICAL RESPONSE: Discuss applied behavior analysis.

There are six steps to setting up and using applied behavior analysis in the classroom: 1) identify target behavior(s) and reinforcer(s); 2) establish a baseline for the target behavior; 3) choose a reinforcer and criteria for reinforcement; 4) if necessary, choose a punisher and criteria for punishment; 5) observe behavior during program implementation and compare it to baseline; and 6) when the program is working, reduce the frequency of reinforcement.

Home-based reinforcement strategies and daily report card programs (a type of home-based reinforcement strategy) service individual students. With home-based programs, teachers give students a daily or weekly report card (contract) to take home and parents are instructed to provide special privileges or rewards to students on the basis of these reports.

Group contingency is a reinforcement program in which an entire group is rewarded on the basis of the behavior of each of the group members.

2. KEY CONCEPTS, PRINCIPLES, AND THEORIES

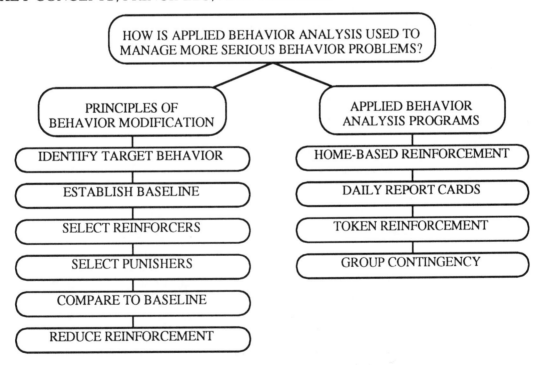

VI. HOW CAN SERIOUS DISCIPLINE PROBLEMS BE PREVENTED?

1. SELF-CHECK ITEM: Describe how you would prevent serious discipline problems.

Develop and defend a plan for preventing serious discipline problems.

TYPICAL RESPONSE: Develop a plan.

1. Enforce classroom rules and practices consistently and fairly.
2. Accommodate instruction to meet the diverse needs of all learners.
3. Practice prevention first, then intervention.
4. Involve parents.
5. Judiciously apply consequences.

2. KEY CONCEPTS, PRINCIPLES, AND THEORIES

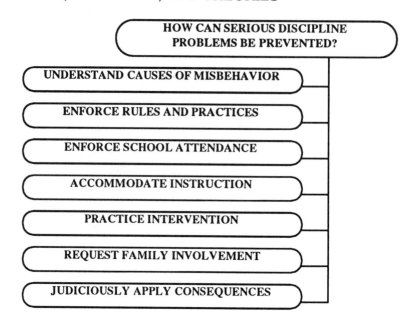

HOW CAN SERIOUS DISCIPLINE PROBLEMS BE PREVENTED?

UNDERSTAND CAUSES OF MISBEHAVIOR

ENFORCE RULES AND PRACTICES

ENFORCE SCHOOL ATTENDANCE

ACCOMMODATE INSTRUCTION

PRACTICE INTERVENTION

REQUEST FAMILY INVOLVEMENT

JUDICIOUSLY APPLY CONSEQUENCES

FOR YOUR ENJOYMENT

This section of the study guide includes suggestions for enriching your understanding of a chapter heading you have mastered. You will find information on activities related to the heading and suggestions for research papers, interviews, or presentation.

I. WHAT IS AN EFFECTIVE LEARNING ENVIRONMENT?

1. Interview teachers about their strategies for maintaining an effective learning environment. Ask them about the rules they have for their classes and the consequences for breaking rules.

II. WHAT IS THE IMPACT OF TIME ON LEARNING?

1. For a research paper, review the literature on "time on-task" behaviors.

III. WHAT PRACTICES CONTRIBUTE TO EFFECTIVE CLASSROOM MANAGEMENT?

1. Create a list of classroom rules to be discussed with your students during the first day of class.

2. Discuss the advantages and disadvantages of having students make their own rules for the class.

3. For a research project, review the literature on establishing rules during the first days of class.

IV.   WHAT ARE SOME STRATEGIES FOR MANAGING ROUTINE MISBEHAVIORS?

1. For a research paper, review the literature on classroom management.

V.   HOW IS APPLIED BEHAVIOR ANALYSIS USED TO MANAGE MORE SERIOUS BEHAVIOR PROBLEMS?

1. For a research paper, review the literature on applied behavior analysis.

IV.   HOW CAN SERIOUS DISCIPLINE PROBLEMS BE PREVENTED?

1. Discuss with other students your concerns about classroom management.

SELF-ASSESSMENT

DIRECTIONS: Below are questions related to the main ideas presented in the chapter. Correct answers or typical responses can be found at the end of the study guide.

1. Which of the following refers to methods used to prevent behavior problems and disruptions?

    A. management
    B. discipline
    C. learning environment
    D. instruction

2. According to research, which of the following strategies would be most likely to increase student achievement?

    A. Increase allocated time by 10 percent above what is normal.
    B. Increase engaged time to 100 percent of the allocated classroom time.
    C. Increase engaged time by 10 percent above what is normal.
    D. Decrease allocated time by late starts and early finishes.

3. Engaged time is synonymous with

    A. time on task.
    B. allocated time.
    C. momentum.
    D. overlapping.

4. Match each of the following terms with its definition.

_____ monitoring the behavior of all students and responding when necessary

_____ using questioning strategies that hold the attention of all students

_____ maintaining the flow of instruction in spite of small interruptions

_____ involving all students in all parts of a lecture or discussion

A. accountability

B. group alerting

C. withitness

D. overlapping

5. All of the following statements about class rules are accurate except

    A. class rules should be few in numbers.
    B. class rules should be seen as fair by students.
    C. class rules should be clearly explained and deliberately taught to students.
    D. class rules should be created by the teacher and students together.

6. According to the principle of least intervention, in which order should the following management methods be used in dealing with discipline problems?

    A. prevention
    B. consequences
    C. nonverbal cues
    D. verbal reminders
    E. praising appropriate behaviors

7. Sequence the following steps of a behavior management program in the order in which they should be used.

    A. Select and use reinforcers and, if necessary, punishers.
    B. Establish a baseline for the target behavior.
    C. Phase out reinforcement.
    D. Identify the target behavior and its reinforcer(s).

8. Daily report cards, group contingency programs, home-based reinforcement programs, and individual behavior management programs are all based on

    A. assertive discipline practices.
    B. delinquency prevention.
    C. behavioral learning theory.
    D. the principle of least intervention.

9. Discuss ethical considerations in the use of individual and group behavior management programs.

10. Explain how you would prevent the following misbehaviors: speaking out of turn, teasing, physical fighting.

PRACTICE TEST ANSWERS

1. Prevent and respond to misbehavior, use class time well, create an atmosphere that is conducive to interest and inquiry, permit the use of activities that engage students' minds and imaginations, present well organized lessons, use incentives for learning effectively, accommodate instruction to students' needs.

2. True; Lost time is the result of any activity that substitutes for actual instruction time.

3. True; On time starts to a lesson that continue until the allocated time for completion result from, at least in part, being over-prepared.

4. False; Interruptions, even minor ones, directly cut into instruction time and disrupt momentum.

5. Teach engaging lessons, maintain momentum, maintain smoothness of instruction, manage transitions, and maintain group focus.

6. Withit teachers are aware of students' behaviors at all times. They seem to have eyes in the back of their heads.

7. Overlapping refers to the teacher's ability to attend to interruptions or behavior problems while continuing with a lesson or other instructional activity.

8. Mock participation results from an overemphasis on engaged time—to the detriment of learning—rather than engaging instruction.

9. True; Teachers at the elementary level need to help students understand what school rules exist and what is required of them.

10. True; Teachers of middle and secondary students need to help students become self-regulated in observing rules.

11. True; Evertson and Emmer found that establishing routines during the first days of school were critical to making classrooms effective learning environments.

12. Class rules should be few in number, they should make sense and appear fair to students, and they should be clearly explained and intentionally taught.

13. Keep high traffic areas free of congestion. Be sure students can be easily seen by the teacher. Keep frequently used teaching materials and student supplies readily available. Be certain students can see instructional presentations and displays.

14. False; Teacher behaviors associated with high time on-task were also associated with fewer serious behavior problems.

15. True; Most classroom behavior problems are minor.

16. Principle of least intervention

17. 1. prevent misbehavior 2. use nonverbal cues 3. praise appropriate behaviors
4. praise other students 5. use verbal reminders 6. use repeated verbal reminders
7. apply consequences

18. D; Group contingency is a strategy in which the entire class is rewarded for its
members' appropriate behavior.

19. 1. Identify target behaviors and reinforcers. 2. Establish a baseline for the target
behavior. 3. Choose a reinforcer and criteria for reinforcement. 4. If necessary, choose a
punisher and criteria for punishment. 5. Observe the behavior during program
implementation and compare it to the baseline. 6. When program is working, reduce the
frequency of reinforcement.

20. A, B, C; daily report card, token reinforcement, group contingency

21. True; Research shows that boys engage in serious misbehaviors far more often than
do girls.

22. True; Students who do not experience success in school see the rewards for behaving
to be small.

23. False; Expectations that students will conform to school rules must be consistently
expressed.

24. 1. enforcing rules and practices 2. enforcing school attendance 3. accommodating
instruction 4. practicing intervention 5. requesting family involvement 6. judiciously
applying consequences

12
EXCEPTIONAL LEARNERS

CHAPTER OVERVIEW

This chapter focuses on the idea that schools are responsible for finding ways to meet the needs of each student in a regular classroom setting, to the extent that it is possible. Described below are some exceptionalities that individuals may have and programs that have been effective in meeting their needs.

Exceptional learners are defined as those students who have mental retardation, learning disabilities, communication disorders, emotional and behavioral disorders, physical impairments, or giftedness.

Exceptional learners have their needs met through the Education For All Handicapped Act and the Americans with Disabilities Act.

Exceptional learners are mainstreamed into the least restrictive environment possible.

CHAPTER OUTLINE

I. WHO ARE EXCEPTIONAL LEARNERS?
- A. Types of Exceptionalities and Number of Students Served
- B. Students with Mental Retardation
- C. Students with Learning Disabilities
- D. Students with Communications Disorders
- E. Students with Emotional and Behavioral Disorders
- F. Students with Sensory, Physical, and Health Impairments
- G. Students Who Are Gifted and Talented

II. WHAT IS SPECIAL EDUCATION?
- A. Public Law 94-142 and IDEA
- B. An Array of Special Education Services

III. WHAT ARE MAINSTREAMING AND INCLUSION?
- A. Research on Mainstreaming and Inclusion
- B. Adapting Instruction
- C. Teaching Learning Strategies and Megacognitive Awareness
- D. Prevention and Early Intervention
- E. Computers and Students with Disabilities
- F. Buddy System and Peer Tutoring
- G. Special Education Teams
- H. Social Integration of Students with Disabilities

PRACTICE TEST

DIRECTIONS: Each chapter heading listed below is followed by a series of related questions worth a total of ten points. Respond to each question, check your answers with those found at the end of the chapter, then determine your score. Consider nine points to be mastery.

For those headings on which you do not score at least nine points, turn to the FOR YOUR INFORMATION section for corrective instruction. For those headings on which you do score at least nine points, turn to the FOR YOUR ENJOYMENT section for enrichment activities.

I. WHO ARE EXCEPTIONAL LEARNERS?

Sentence Completion

1. (1 point) _____ is the term used to describe students who exhibit one or more characteristics that affect their ability to learn.

2. (1 point) _____ is the exceptionality that is characterized by significantly below average intellectual functioning, which may limit communication, self-care, social skills, health, or safety. ___

3. (1 point) _____ is the exceptionality that is not a single condition, but a wide variety of disabilities stemming from brain or central nervous system dysfunction characterized by difficulties in listening, speaking, reading, writing, reasoning, or computing.

4. (1 point) _____ is the exceptionality that is characterized by problems with speech and language.

5. (1 point) _____ is the exceptionality characterized by problems with learning, interpersonal relationships, and controlling feelings and behavior.

6. (1 point) _____ is the exceptionality that refers to an inability to see or hear or otherwise receive information through the body's senses.

Short Answer/Essay

7. (2 points) List one type of physical disorder and one type of health disorder.

_____

_____

8. (2 points) Define "giftedness."

_____

_____

II. WHAT IS SPECIAL EDUCATION?

9. (1 point) _____

True or False

Special education refers to any program provided for learners with disabilities instead of, or in addition to, the regular classroom program.

10. (1 point) _____

Sentence Completion

_____ is the law that prescribes the services that all learners with disabilities must receive.

11. (1 point) _____

_____ is, according to federal law, the term given to the placement status of students with special needs.

12. (1 point) _____

_____ is the term that refers to the placement of students who have special needs with their peers who do not have special needs for as much of their educational program as possible.

13. (1 point) _____

_____ is the plan that describes a student's educational needs and delineates a special course of action.

14. (5 points)

Short Answer/Essay

Complete the following continuum of services provided by school districts.

1. direct or indirect consultation support for the general education teacher _____
2. _____
3. _____
4. _____
5. _____
6. _____
7. student is placed at home or is hospitalized _____

III. WHAT ARE MAINSTREAMING AND INCLUSION?

15. (1 point) _____

Multiple Choice

All of the following are advantages of using computers to instruct students with special needs except

A. computers foster individualized instruction.
B. computers provide immediate feedback.
C. computers serve as motivators.
D. computers keep the rate of presentation steady.

16. (1 point) _____

Which of the following statements justifies the use of "buddy systems" or "peer tutoring?"

A. Buddy systems help teachers with instruction and evaluation of achievement.
B. Buddy systems assist teachers with non-instructional needs (e.g., note taking for students with hearing impairments).
C. Peer tutoring is an efficient method of providing instructional assistance that requires very little training.

Short Answer/Essay

17. (1 point)   List one advantage of inclusion programs.

_____

18. (1 point)   List one advantage of pull-out programs.

_____

19. (2 point)   Describe the type of expertise that regular education and special education teachers can bring together to solve problems for students with special needs.

_____

_____

20. (4 points)   List four ways that teachers can foster the social integration of students with special needs into the regular classroom.

_____

_____

_____

_____

SCORING	POINTS NEEDED FOR MASTERY	POINTS RECEIVED
I. WHO ARE EXCEPTIONAL LEARNERS?	9	
II. WHAT IS SPECIAL EDUCATION?	9	
III. WHAT ARE MAINSTREAMING AND INCLUSION?	9	

FOR YOUR INFORMATION

This section of the study guide includes suggestions for further study of the information you have not yet mastered. You will find information on: 1) typical responses to the SELF-CHECK item(s) from the text; and 2) key concepts, principles, and theories addressed in the text chapter.

I. WHO ARE EXCEPTIONAL LEARNERS?

1. SELF-CHECK ITEM: Define *learners with exceptionalities* and distinguish between *disability* and *handicap*. Give examples of each and explain why labeling has limitations. Then define and describe the characteristics of each of the following concepts: mental retardation, giftedness, physical disability, vision loss, hearing loss, learning disability, emotional/behavior disorder, communication disorder, speech disorder, language disorder, autism, traumatic brain injury.

TYPICAL RESPONSE: Discuss terms, disorders associated with exceptionalities.

The term exceptionality refers to students who are said to exhibit characteristics that somehow affect their ability to learn. A disability is a functional limitation a person has that interferes with his or her physical or cognitive abilities. A handicap is a condition imposed on a person with disabilities by society, the physical environment, or her or his attitude. Labeling can be harmful because it (unintentionally) stigmatizes, dehumanizes, and segregates those individuals being labeled.

Mental retardation refers to substantial limitations in intellectual functioning that affect an individual's ability to communicate, socialize, take care of himself or herself, function academically, or work.

Learning disabilities refer to difficulties in the acquisition and use of listening, speaking, reading, writing, reasoning, or computing. This wide range of conditions is thought to stem from some dysfunction of the brain or central nervous system. Included as a learning disability is attention deficit hyperactivity disorder (ADHD).

Communication disorders refer to problems associated with speech and language. Speech disorders are those associated with the formation and sequencing of sounds and include articulation (or phonological) disorders, such as omissions, distortions, or substitutions of sounds. Language disorders are those associated with the communication of ideas using symbols and include receptive and expressive difficulties.

Emotional disorders refer to problems associated with learning, interpersonal relationships, and controlling feelings and behaviors. Conduct disorders, while under the category of emotional and behavioral disabilities, in themselves, are not recognized for special education services.

Sensory impairments refer to the inability to see or hear or otherwise receive information through the body's senses. Visual and hearing impairments are two types of sensory disorders.

Physical disabilities include cerebral palsy, a motor impairment caused by brain damage, and seizure disorders, caused by an abnormal amount of electrical discharge to the brain.

Giftedness refers to those who are identified as possessing demonstrated or potential abilities that give evidence of high performance capabilities in areas such as intellectual, creative, academic, or leadership pursuits.

2. KEY CONCEPTS, PRINCIPLES, AND THEORIES

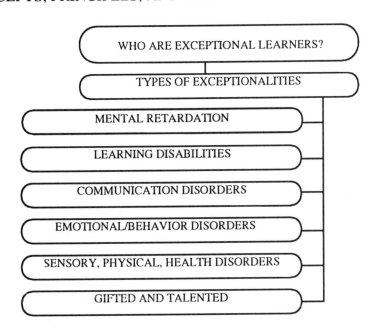

WHO ARE EXCEPTIONAL LEARNERS?

TYPES OF EXCEPTIONALITIES

MENTAL RETARDATION

LEARNING DISABILITIES

COMMUNICATION DISORDERS

EMOTIONAL/BEHAVIOR DISORDERS

SENSORY, PHYSICAL, HEALTH DISORDERS

GIFTED AND TALENTED

II. WHAT IS SPECIAL EDUCATION?

1. SELF-CHECK ITEM: Define *special education*. Trace the history of federal laws—Public Law 94-142, PL 99-457, PL 101-476, and PL 105-17—that regulate the education of students with special needs. Define least restricted environment and describe the educational environments in which students with special needs are placed. What other types of services are available? List the minimum information that an Individualized Education Program (IEP) must contain; then list the steps you would take to prepare one.

TYPICAL RESPONSE: Define special education and describe the laws and services provided through special education programs.

Special education refers to any program provided for students with special needs instead of, or in addition to, the regular education program. Public Law 94-142, the Education for All Handicapped Act prescribes that services must be given to students with special education needs at the public's expense. Public Law 99-457 extends the entitlement to free, appropriate programs for children who are infants to five years old. Public Law 101-476, the Individuals with Disabilities Education Act, requires schools to plan for the transition of adolescents with disabilities into further education or employment starting at age 16.

Least restrictive environment refers to a provision in the law (IDEA) that requires students with special needs to be educated in a regular education classroom to the maximum extent appropriate.

There are five main kinds of placement extended to students with special needs: 1) regular classroom placement; 2) consultation and itinerant services; 3) resource room placement; 4) special class placement with part time mainstreaming; and 5) self-contained special education. In addition to these services, schools often provide psychologists, speech and language therapists, physical and occupational therapists, social workers and pupil personnel workers, and homebound instruction.

The steps you would take to prepare an Individualized Education Program (IEP) must include the following:
A. initial referral
B. screening and assessment
C. writing the IEP to include:
    1) a statement indicating the individual's present level of performance
    2) goals indicating anticipated progress during the year
    3) intermediate (shorter term) instructional objectives
    4) a statement of the specific special education and related services to be provided as well as the extent to which the student will participate in regular education programs
    5) the projected date for the initiation of services and anticipated duration of services
    6. evaluation criteria and procedures for measuring progress toward goals on an annual basis

2. KEY CONCEPTS, PRINCIPLES, AND THEORIES

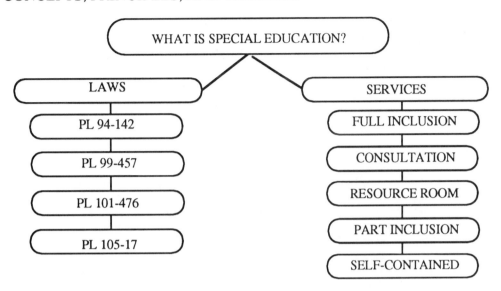

III. WHAT ARE MAINSTREAMING AND INCLUSION?

1. SELF-CHECK ITEM: Define *mainstreaming* and *inclusion*. Discuss research findings on the effectiveness of mainstreaming and full inclusion approaches. Describe the most effective strategies for accommodating instruction for classes with mainstreamed students. How do computers, buddy systems, peer tutoring, special education teams, and social integration approaches assist students with special needs?

TYPICAL RESPONSE: Define and discuss the effects of mainstreaming and inclusion.

> Mainstreaming is the integration of students with special needs into the general classroom. Inclusion (full inclusion) places students who have disabilities into the general class with support services.

> Mainstreaming requires that students with special needs be placed in the least restrictive environment possible. In general, students excel at a somewhat higher degree when they are placed in the regular education classroom with individual education plans. Highly structured resource room programs have also been found to be effective for those students who need specialized assistance. Some of the most effective programs for working with students who have special needs include cooperative learning groups, computer assisted instruction, buddy systems, peer tutoring, team consultation, and social integration.

> Computers provide individualized instruction (e.g., method of delivery, type and frequency of reinforcement, rate of presentation, and level of instruction), give immediate feedback, and hold the attention of students.

> Buddy systems help meet the needs of students with disabilities by allowing regular education students to assist with non-instructional tasks, such as providing directions, delivering cues when needed, note taking, and reading.

> Peer tutors, who must be carefully trained, can provide assistance by modeling, explaining, and giving positive and corrective feedback. Research shows that both parties involved in the peer tutoring benefit.

Team consultation brings together the expertise of both the regular education teacher and the special education teacher. The regular education teacher is the expert on how the classroom is organized and operates on a day-to-day basis, the curriculum of the classroom, and what expectations are placed on students for performance. The special educator is the expert on the characteristics of a particular group of disabilities, the special learning and behavioral strengths and deficits of the students who have these disabilities, and techniques for adapting regular classroom instruction.

Social integration requires that the teacher's attitude toward students with special needs be positive and appropriate as she or he serves as a model for the regular education students. Cooperative learning groups also work to socially integrate a classroom.

2. KEY CONCEPTS, PRINCIPLES, AND THEORIES

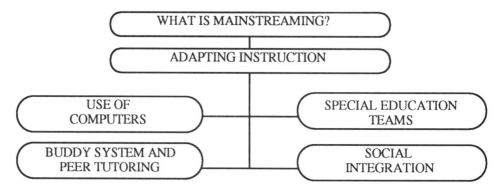

FOR YOUR ENJOYMENT

This section of the study guide includes suggestions for enriching your understanding of a chapter heading you have mastered. You will find information on activities related to the heading and suggestions for research papers, interviews, or presentations.

I. WHO ARE EXCEPTIONAL LEARNERS?

1. For a research topic, review the literature on exceptional learners.

II. WHAT IS SPECIAL EDUCATION?

1. Interview a principal, a special education director, and a teacher about the special education services provided to students with special needs.

III. WHAT IS MAINSTREAMING?

1. Conduct a research study about the attitudes of various school personnel regarding the effectiveness of inclusion.

CHAPTER TWELVE: SELF-ASSESSMENT

DIRECTIONS: Below are questions related to the main ideas presented in the chapter. Correct answers or typical responses can be found at the end of the study guide.

1. Explain the difference between a handicap and a disability.

2. Approximately what percentage of all students ages 6 to 17 have mental retardation?

    A. 1.2 percent
    B. 5.8 percent
    C. 8.3 percent
    D. 10.1 percent

3. Match the following description with its exceptionality type.

    _____ difficulties with expressive and receptive communications

    _____ general term that refers to performing below what an IQ would predict

    _____ omissions, distortions, and substitutions of sounds

    _____ anxiety, phobias, aggression, or acute shyness

    A. emotional disorders

    B. language disorder

    C. learning disabilities

    D. speech disorder

4. Problems with the ability to see or hear or otherwise receive information are labeled

    A. sensory impairments.
    B. learning disabilities.
    C. attention deficit disorders.
    D. emotional and behavioral disorders.

5. List two common options for adapting education programs to the needs of students who are gifted and talented.

6. Match the federal law regarding the education of students with special needs with its description.

    _____ This federal law, enacted in 1975, requires that special services be provided to all students in need.

    _____ This federal law, enacted in 1986, extends free, appropriate education to children ages three to five.

    _____ This federal law, enacted in 1990, requires schools to plan for the transition of adolescents with disabilities into future education or employment.

    _____ This federal law, enacted in 1997, raises educational expectations for students with disabilities and increases parental and teacher involvement.

    A. P.L. 101-476

    B. P.L. 94-142

    C. P.L. 99-457

    D. P.L. 105-17

7. Rank the following special education placements in order from the least restrictive (1) to most restrictive (4).

_____ resource room
_____ part-time mainstreaming into the general education classroom
_____ self-contained special-education classroom
_____ general education classroom

8. List the steps followed when developing an Individualized Education Program.

9. What problems or benefits may occur when students with special needs are included in the general education classroom?

10. In some areas of the country, minority group students account for two-thirds of the enrollment in classes for students with mental disabilities. What are some reasons for this overrepresentation?

PRACTICE TEST ANSWERS

1. Exceptional learner

2. Mental retardation

3. Learning disabilities

4. Communication disorder

5. Emotional and behavior disorder

6. Sensory disorder

7. Physical disorders include cerebral palsy, spina bifida, spinal cord injury, and muscular dystrophy. Health disorders include AIDS, seizure disorders, diabetes, cystic fibrosis, sickle cell anemia, and bodily damage from chemical addiction, child abuse, or attempted suicide.

8. Giftedness refers to individuals who are identified as possessing demonstrated or potential abilities that give evidence of high performance capabilities in intellectual, creative, specific academic, or leadership.

9. True; Special education refers to any services or programs provided for individuals with disabilities instead of, or in addition to, regular classroom programs.

10. PL 94-142; Education for the Handicapped Act

11. Least restrictive; The provisions of PL 94-142 state that individuals with special needs must be assigned to the least restrictive placement appropriate to their needs.

12. Mainstreaming; Mainstreaming places students with special needs with their regular classroom peers for as much of their education program as possible.

13. Individualized Education Program (IEP); An IEP describes the student's problem and identifies possible solutions.

14. 1) direct or indirect consultation support for general education teacher; 2) special education up to one hour per day; 3) special education one to three hours per day, resource room; 4) special education more than three hours per day, self-contained special education; 5) special day school; 6) special residential school; 6) home or hospital

15. D; Computers allow for variance in the rate of presentation to meet the needs of the student.

16. B; Buddy systems involve the teaming of two students, one requiring special services, to work together on non-instructional tasks.

17. Inclusion programs encourage effective partnerships between regular and special educators. Inclusion removes the stigma associated with students who are segregated from those in a regular program.

18. Pull out programs ensure that those educators who work with students with special needs will be trained to do so.

19. The regular classroom teacher is the expert on how the class is organized and operates on a day-to-day basis, the curriculum, and the expectations for performance. The special education teacher is the expert on the types of handicapping conditions a student might have, the strengths and needs involved with the disability, and instruction techniques for adapting curriculum.

20. 1) model a caring attitude; 2) use an IEP; 3) have expectations; 4) use cooperative learning; 5) use peer tutors; 6) provide participation opportunities
7) allow for the development of friendships

13
ASSESSING STUDENT LEARNING

CHAPTER OVERVIEW

The major objective of this chapter is to show the relationships among planning, teaching, and evaluating student achievement. Previous chapters have discussed effective teaching components. This chapter discusses the planning and evaluating of instructional objectives. Listed below is an overview of the important points of the chapter.

Assessing student learning involves the appropriate use of instructional objectives.

Assessing student learning is important because it provides feedback to students, parents, and teachers, serves as evidence of teacher and program accountability, and motivates students' efforts.

Assessing student learning is accomplished through the use of formative or summative evaluations and criterion-referenced or norm-referenced measures.

Assessing student learning is accomplished through the use of well-constructed tests using multiple choice, true-false, completion, matching, short essay, and problem solving items.

Assessing student learning can involve the use of portfolios and other types of performance assessments.

CHAPTER OUTLINE

I. WHAT ARE INSTRUCTIONAL OBJECTIVES AND HOW ARE THEY USED?
   A. Planning Lesson Objectives
   B. Linking Objectives and Assessment
   C. Using Taxonomies of Instructional Objectives
   D. Research on Instructional Objectives

II. WHY IS EVALUATION IMPORTANT?
   A. Evaluation as Feedback
   B. Evaluation as Information
   C. Evaluation as Incentive

III. HOW IS STUDENT LEARNING EVALUATED?
   A. Formative and Summative Evaluations
   B. Norm-Referenced, Criterion-Referenced, and Authentic Evaluations
   C. Matching Evaluation Strategies with Goals

IV. HOW ARE TESTS CONSTRUCTED?
   A. Principles of Achievement Testing
   B. Using a Table of Specifications
   C. Writing Objective Test Items

D. Writing and Evaluating Essay Tests
E. Writing and Evaluating Problem Solving Items

V. WHAT ARE PORTFOLIO AND PERFORMANCE ASSESSMENTS?
   A. Portfolio Assessment
   B. Performance Assessment
   C. How Well Do Performance Assessments Work?
   D. Scoring Rubrics for Performance Assessments

PRACTICE TEST

DIRECTIONS: Each chapter heading listed below is followed by a series of related questions worth a total of ten points. Respond to each question, check your answers with those found at the end of the chapter, then determine your score. Consider nine points per heading to be mastery.

For those headings on which you do not score at least nine points, turn to the FOR YOUR INFORMATION section for corrective instruction. For those headings on which you do score at least nine points, turn to the FOR YOUR ENJOYMENT section for enrichment activities.

I. WHAT ARE INSTRUCTIONAL OBJECTIVES AND HOW ARE THEY USED?

True or False

1. (1 point) _____ Setting out objectives at the beginning of a course or unit of study is an essential step in providing a framework for teaching and evaluating.

2. (1 point) _____ Instructional objectives are statements of what the learner will be like following a unit of instruction.

Multiple Choice

3. (1 point) _____ Which of the following lists represents the parts of a behavioral objective?

   A. performance, behavior, action
   B. cognitive, affective, psychomotor
   C. performance, condition, criteria
   D. affective, condition, action

Matching

4. (3 points) _____ domain that focuses on attitudes such as receiving, responding, and valuing   A. cognitive

                                                                                                              B. affective

            _____ domain that focuses on physical skill development   C. psychomotor

            _____ domain that focuses on mental operations

5. (3 points)   *Short Answer/Essay*
List the three steps involved in a task analysis.

_____

_____

_____

6. (1 point)   Describe the process of "backward planning."

_____

_____

II. WHY IS EVALUATION IMPORTANT?

7. (1 point) _____   *True or False*
Evaluation refers to all of the means used in schools to formally measure student performance.

8. (3 points)   *Short Answer/Essay*
Give three examples of ways to evaluate students.

_____

_____

_____

9. (6 points)   Identify six purposes for evaluating students.

_____

_____

_____

_____

_____

_____

III. HOW IS STUDENT LEARNING EVALUATED?

10. (1 point) _____   *True or False*
The most effective way to measure objectives is through written, formal evaluations.

11. (4 points) _____   *Matching*
form of evaluation that answers the question, "How are you doing?"

      _____   form of evaluation that focuses on asssessing students' mastery of skills, based on some predetermined standard

      _____   form of evaluation that focuses on a student's placement within the group

      _____   form of evaluation that answers the question, "How did you do?"

A. formative

B. summative

C. norm-referenced

D. criterion-referenced

12. (2 points) *Short Answer/Essay*
List two types of alternative assessments.

_____

_____

13. (3 points) List three problems with using grades as incentives.

_____

_____

_____

IV. HOW ARE TESTS CONSTRUCTED?

14. (1 point) _____
Sentence Completion
One way to assure that objectives are being tested is to construct a matrix of the objectives and levels of learning.

15. (6 points) *Short Answer/Essay*
List the six principles to follow when constructing achievement tests.

_____

_____

_____

_____

_____

_____

16. (3 points) List three types of items used when writing objective tests.

_____

_____

_____

V. WHAT ARE PORTFOLIO AND PERFORMANCE ASSESSMENTS?

17. (1 point) _____
True or False
Portfolio assessments are a collection of the student's work in an area showing growth, self-reflection, and achievement.

18. (1 point) _____
The research evidence about the reliability of portfolios is promising.

19. (1 point) _____
Assessments of students' abilities to perform tasks, not just the knowledge that is necessary, are called performance assessments.

184

20. (3 points)   What are three disadvantages to performance assessments?

_____
_____
_____

21. (4 points)   List the steps associated with a performance assessment.

_____
_____
_____
_____

SCORING	POINTS NEEDED FOR MASTERY	POINTS RECEIVED
I. WHAT ARE INSTRUCTIONAL OBJECTIVES AND HOW ARE THEY USED?	9	
II. WHY IS EVALUATION IMPORTANT?	9	
III. HOW IS STUDENT LEARNING EVALUATED?	9	
IV. HOW ARE TESTS CONSTRUCTED?	9	
V. WHAT ARE PORTFOLIO AND PERFORMANCE ASSESSMENTS?	9	

FOR YOUR INFORMATION

This section of the study guide includes suggestions for further study of the information you have not yet mastered. You will find information on: 1) typical responses to the SELF-CHECK item(s) from the text; and 2) key concepts, principles, and theories addressed in the text chapter.

I. WHAT ARE INSTRUCTIONAL OBJECTIVES AND HOW ARE THEY USED?

1. SELF-CHECK ITEM: Practice writing instructional objectives, perform a task analysis, and use backward planning to create a unit of study. Develop a behavior content matrix with one cognitive objective and one affective objective.

TYPICAL RESPONSE: Write instructional objectives.

Given a map of the United States, students will label all the state capitals.

Using the appropriate tools and materials, students will create a piece of art.

Students will select, read, and interpret a poem.

Students will calculate the diameters of circles.

Without error, students will perform each step of cardiopulmonary resuscitation.

Students will identify the planets of the solar system.
Students will take a position on a current social issue, using facts to support their beliefs.

TYPICAL RESPONSE: Perform a task analysis and use backward planning.

Course objective: The students will calculate using addition, subtraction, multiplication, and division.
Unit objective: The students will calculate using division.
Lesson objective: The students will calculate double digit numbers with remainders.

identify prerequisite skills: subtraction and multiplication with renaming; division

identify component skills: estimating, dividing, multiplying, subtracting, checking,
                                    bringing down the next digit, and repeating

assemble into final skill: integrate sub-skills

TYPICAL RESPONSE: Develop a behavior content matrix.

TYPE OF OBJECTIVE	EXAMPLE
cognitive	Students will discriminate between offensive and defensive plays.
affective	Students will accept responsibly for their roles as part of a team.
psychomotor	Students will perform the physical skills necessary to participate in a game.

2. KEY CONCEPTS, PRINCIPLES, AND THEORIES

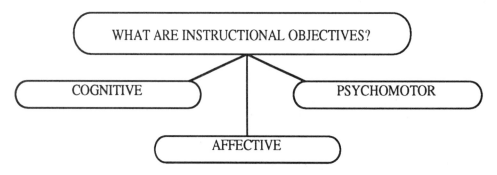

WHAT ARE INSTRUCTIONAL OBJECTIVES?

COGNITIVE   PSYCHOMOTOR

AFFECTIVE

II. WHY IS EVALUATION IMPORTANT?

1. SELF-CHECK ITEM: List the six primary purposes for evaluating students' learning. Give an example of each purpose.

TYPICAL RESPONSE: Identify and give examples of evaluation purposes.

PURPOSE	EXAMPLE
feedback to student	specific written assessments of strengths and weaknesses
feedback to teacher	evaluate instructional effectiveness

information to parents	reports of progress (e.g., report cards)
information for selection	placement, tracking (e.g., college prep or vocational)
information for accountability	standardized tests of overall achievement of students
incentive to increase student effort	motivate students with sound, consistent, clear, reliable, frequent, and challenging evaluations

2. KEY CONCEPTS, PRINCIPLES, AND THEORIES

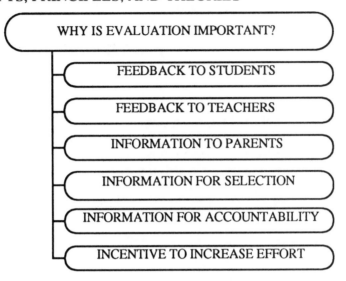

WHY IS EVALUATION IMPORTANT?

FEEDBACK TO STUDENTS

FEEDBACK TO TEACHERS

INFORMATION TO PARENTS

INFORMATION FOR SELECTION

INFORMATION FOR ACCOUNTABILITY

INCENTIVE TO INCREASE EFFORT

III. HOW IS STUDENT LEARNING EVALUATED?

1. SELF-CHECK ITEM: Construct a four-square matrix comparing formative and summative testing on one axis and norm-referenced and criterion-referenced on the other axis. In each square, write a brief description of optimal conditions for using each combination.

TYPICAL RESPONSE: Construct a matrix.

	FORMATIVE EVALUATION	SUMMATIVE EVALUATION
NORM-REFERENCED MEASURES	comparison of students to each other to discover strengths and weaknesses for making corrections in instruction	comparison of students to each other to assign grades (on the curve, percentiles) or other final assessments
CRITERION-REFERENCED MEASURES	comparison of students to expectations of identified objectives to discover strengths and weaknesses for making corrections in instruction	comparison of students to expectations of identified objectives to assign grades (points, percentages) or other final assessments

2. KEY CONCEPTS, PRINCIPLES, AND THEORIES

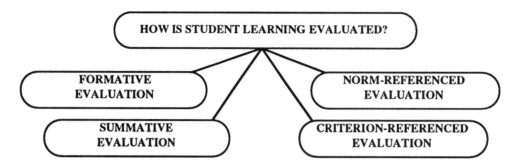

IV. HOW ARE TESTS CONSTRUCTED?

1. SELF-CHECK ITEM: Write a variety of test items, including multiple choice, true-false, completion, matching, short essay, and problem-solving questions.

TYPICAL RESPONSE: Write test items.

OBJECTIVE	TEST ITEM
Students will name state capitals.	Which of the following cities is the capital of Minnesota? A. Minneapolis B. Indianapolis C. St. Paul D. Bismarck
Students will identify the elementary particles of an atom.	T F Neutrons are negatively charged particles of electricity.
Students will recall famous presidents.	The first president of the United States was _____.

Students will identify composers and their major works.	__ Composer of *Emperor Concerto*. A. Bach
	__ Composer of *1812 Overture*. B. Beethoven
	__ Composer of *New World Symphony*. C. Copland
	                                                          D. Dvorak
	                                                          E. Tchiakovsky

Students will describe the major causes of air pollution.	List and briefly describe three major causes of air pollution using a five paragraph format.
Students will calculate problems of probability.	If a person is chosen at random from the world population, what is the probability that he or she is from the United States?

2. KEY CONCEPTS, PRINCIPLES, AND THEORIES

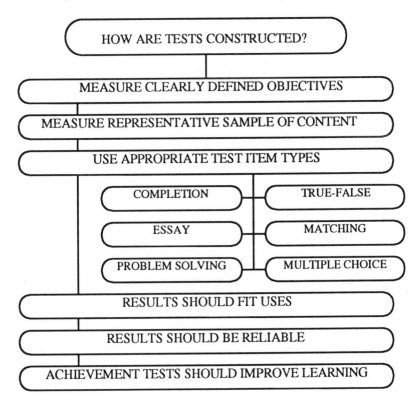

HOW ARE TESTS CONSTRUCTED?

MEASURE CLEARLY DEFINED OBJECTIVES

MEASURE REPRESENTATIVE SAMPLE OF CONTENT

USE APPROPRIATE TEST ITEM TYPES

COMPLETION — TRUE-FALSE

ESSAY — MATCHING

PROBLEM SOLVING — MULTIPLE CHOICE

RESULTS SHOULD FIT USES

RESULTS SHOULD BE RELIABLE

ACHIEVEMENT TESTS SHOULD IMPROVE LEARNING

V. WHAT ARE PORTFOLIO AND PERFORMANCE ASSESSMENTS?

1. SELF-CHECK ITEM: Make a list of items that might be included in a portfolio. Create rubrics for a specific performance.

TYPICAL RESPONSE: What is a portfolio. Create rubrics.

> Portfolio assessment is a collection of the student's work in an area showing growth, self-reflection, and achievement. Items included in a portfolio may include journal entries, book reports, artwork, computer printouts, or papers. Performance assessments are typically scored according to rubrics that specify in advance the type of performance that is expected for each rating.

FOR YOUR ENJOYMENT

This section of the study guide includes suggestions for enriching your understanding of a chapter heading you have mastered. You will find information on activities related to the heading and suggestions for research papers, interviews, or presentations.

I. WHAT ARE INSTRUCTIONAL OBJECTIVES AND HOW ARE THEY USED?

1. Practice writing instructional objectives in the cognitive, affective, and psychomotor domains.

2. Compare Bloom's taxonomy of instructional objectives to Gagne's categories of learning outcomes.

II. WHY IS EVALUATION IMPORTANT?

1. Interview teachers, administrators, and students on their perceptions of evaluation. Are their beliefs congruent?

III. HOW IS STUDENT LEARNING EVALUATED?

1. Discuss the advantages and disadvantages of norm-referenced measures and criterion-referenced measures with teachers, administrators, and students.

IV. HOW ARE TESTS CONSTRUCTED?

1. Construct a test for your area of study.

V. WHAT ARE PORTFOLIO AND PERFORMANCE ASSESSMENTS?

1. Create an instrument that can be used to assess learning.

CHAPTER THIRTEEN: SELF-ASSESSMENT

DIRECTIONS: Below are questions related to the main ideas presented in the chapter. Correct answers or typical responses can be found at the end of the study guide.

1. A statement of skills or concepts that students are expected to know or do at the end of some period of instruction is called a(an)

    A. table of specifications.
    B. content matrix.
    C. instructional objective.
    D. taxonomy.

2. For the following objective, label the condition, performance, and criterion.
Given a map of the United States, students will label all of the state capitals.

3. A student is shown a model of a space shuttle and asked to explain what its different components are and how they interact. What type of learning is most clearly being emphasized?

4. What is the term used for the chart showing how a concept or skill will be taught at different cognitive levels in relation to an instructional objective?

    A. task analysis
    B. backward planning
    C. behavior content matrix
    D. table of specifications

5. List six reasons why evaluation is important.

6. According to Gronlund's principles of achievement testing, tests should

    A. include all instructional content.
    B. include all item types.
    C. be free from the confines of instructional objectives.
    D. fit the particular uses that will be made of the results.

7. Match each of the following types of evaluation with its description.

_____ follows conclusion of an instructional unit   A. formative

_____ given during instruction; can guide lesson   B. summative
        presentation

8. Giving feedback to parents on student performance is part of a teacher's job. What type of grading orientation—norm-referenced or criterion-referenced—would be best understood by most parents? How might the choices vary depending on grade level?

9. The purpose of devising a table of specifications in testing is to

    A. indicate the types of learning to be assessed for different instructional objectives.
    B. measure a student's performance against a specified standard.
    C. make comparisons between and among students.
    D. identify conditions of mastery.

10. In a typical portfolio, both subjective and objective measurements are included. Are these equally valid and useful in making educational decisions?

PRACTICE TEST ANSWERS

1. True; Objectives guide instruction and evaluation.

2. True; Objectives are statements of learning intents.

3. C; An instructional objective specifically states a performance and may include a condition and the criteria necessary for successfully completing the objective.

4. B, C, A; affective, psychomotor, cognitive

5. Identify prerequisite skills, identify component skills, and plan how component skills will be assembled into the final performance.

6. Backward planning begins with broad objectives for the course as a whole, then unit objectives and lesson objectives are created.

7. True; Evaluation refers to the process of determining student achievement.

8. Quizzes, written examinations, and grades

9. Feedback to students, feedback to teachers, information to parents, information for selection, information for accountability, and incentive to increase effort

10. False; Different objectives have different purposes; therefore, teachers must choose different types of evaluation to measure achievement.

11. A, D, C, B; Formative evaluations monitor student progress during instruction. Criterion-referenced measures are descriptions of performances that are based on clearly defined learning tasks, outcomes, or standards. Norm-referenced measures are descriptions of performances that are determined by a student's relative position in some group. Summative evaluations determine student progress following instruction.

12. Portfolios and performance assessments

13. Grades are given infrequently, grades are too far removed from performance, grades are usually based on comparative standards

14. Table of specifications

15. Tests should: 1) measure clearly defined objectives; 2) measure a representative sample of the learning task; 3) include appropriate items that measure objectives; 4) fit the particular uses that will be made of the results; 5) be reliable and interpreted with caution; and 6) improve learning.

16. True-false, matching, multiple choice, completion, essay, problem solving

17. True; Portfolios are a collection and evaluation of a student's work over an extended period of time.

18. False; The research evidence is largely disappointing.

19. True; Authentic assessments that involve actual demonstration of knowledge or skills are called performance assessments.

20. 1) They are more expensive that traditional tests. 2) Administering and scoring are difficult. 3) It is not clear that they will solve the problems associated with standardized or traditional tests.

21. 1) Identify a valued education outcome. 2) Develop tasks students can perform to support their learning of the outcome. 3) Identify additional desired education outcomes that are supported by the task. 4) Establish criteria and performance levels for evaluating student performances.

14
STANDARDIZED TESTS AND GRADES

CHAPTER OVERVIEW

The purpose of this chapter is to discuss how and why standardized tests are used, and how scores on these tests can be interpreted and combined with other assessment techniques to make important educational decisions such as assigning grades. Information regarding standardized testing and grading is listed below.

Standardized tests are uniform in content, administration, and scoring; therefore, they allow for the comparison of results across classrooms, schools, and school districts.

Standardized tests measure aptitude, intelligence, and achievement as well as diagnose learning difficulties.

Standardized tests are reported in terms of percentiles, grade equivalents, and standard scores.

Standardized tests must have content, predictive, and construct validity; and, they must be reliable.

CHAPTER OUTLINE

I. WHAT ARE STANDARDIZED TESTS AND HOW ARE THEY USED?
    A. Selection and Placement
    B. Diagnosis
    C. Evaluation
    D. School Improvement
    E. Accountability

II. WHAT TYPES OF STANDARDIZED TESTS ARE GIVEN?
    A. Aptitude Tests
    B. Norm-Referenced Achievement Tests
    C. Criterion-Referenced Achievement Tests

III. HOW ARE STANDARDIZED TESTS INTERPRETED?
    A. Percentile Scores
    B. Grade Equivalent Scores
    C. Standard Scores

IV. WHAT ARE SOME ISSUES CONCERNING STANDARDIZED AND CLASSROOM TESTING?
    A. Validity and Reliability
    B. Test Bias

V. HOW ARE GRADES DETERMINED?
    A. Establishing Grade Criteria
    B. Assigning Letter Grades
    C. Performance Grading
    D. Alternative Grading Systems
    E. Assigning Report Card Grades

PRACTICE TEST

DIRECTIONS: Each chapter heading listed below is followed by a series of related questions worth a total of ten points. Respond to each question, check your answers with those found at the end of the chapter, then determine your score. Consider nine points per heading to be mastery.

For those headings on which you do not score at least nine points, turn to the FOR YOUR INFORMATION section for corrective instruction. For those headings on which you do score at least nine points, turn to the FOR YOUR ENJOYMENT section for enrichment activities.

I. WHAT ARE STANDARDIZED TESTS AND HOW ARE THEY USED?

Short Answer/Essay

1. (10 points)   Describe five uses of standardized tests.

_____
_____
_____
_____
_____
_____
_____
_____
_____
_____
_____

II. WHAT TYPES OF STANDARDIZED TESTS ARE GIVEN?

Matching

2. (3 points) _____ test designed to predict the ability of students to learn or perform particular types of tasks

A. aptitude tests

_____ test of a student's knowledge of a particular content area in which her or his scores are compared with others who were tested

B. norm-referenced tests

_____ test of a student's knowledge of a particular content area in which his or her scores are compared to well specified skills

C. criterion-referenced tests

3. (2 points)

Short Answer/Essay
List two types of aptitude tests.

_____

_____

4. (3 points)

List three types of norm-referenced achievement tests.

_____

_____

_____

5. (2 points)

Describe two ways that criterion-referenced achievement tests differ from norm-referenced achievement tests.

_____

_____

III. HOW ARE STANDARDIZED TEST SCORES INTERPRETED?

6. (1 point) _____

Sentence Completion
are students' raw scores that are translated into percentiles, grade equivalents or normal curve equivalents.

7. (1 point) _____

are scores reported as the percentage of students in the norming group who scored lower than a particular score.

8. (1 point) _____

are scores reported as the average scores obtained by students at particular levels of achievement.

9. (1 point) _____

Multiple Choice
Which of the following terms refers to the statistical measure of the degree of dispersion in a distribution of scores?

A. standard deviation
B. raw score
C. percentile score
D. mean

10. (1 point) _____

What type of curve is produced by a frequency graph of a normal distribution?

A. a curve that is skewed left
B. a curve that is skewed right
C. a bell-shaped curve
D. a curve that is depressed at the mean

11. (1 point) _____ IQ scores are usually presented in which of the following manners?

A. with a mean of 10 and a standard deviation of 1
B. with a mean of 50 and a standard deviation of 5
C. with a mean of 100 and a standard deviation of 15
D. with a mean of 500 and a standard deviation of 50

Short Answer/Essay
12. (2 points) Explain "stanines" and how they are calculated.

_____

_____

13. (2 points) Explain normal curve equivalents.

_____

_____

IV. WHAT ARE SOME ISSUES CONCERNING STANDARDIZED AND CLASSROOM TESTING?

True or False
14. (1 point) _____ The term "validity" refers to the results of a test measuring the type of information purported.

15. (1 point) _____ The term "reliability" refers to the accuracy of the test results.

Matching
16. (3 points) _____ type of validity evidence that relates a test to other similar measures   A. content validity

_____ type of validity evidence that relates a test to future performance   B. predictive validity

_____ type of validity evidence that relates a test to the objectives of a lesson, unit, or course   C. construct validity

Short Answer/Essay
17. (4 points) List four major criticisms of traditional multiple choice standardized tests.

_____

_____

_____

_____

18. (1 point) Describe a type of authentic assessment.

_____

197

V. HOW ARE GRADES DETERMINED?

True or False

19. (1 point) _____ According to Burton, the reason that primary teachers give grades is to inform students of their progress.

20. (1 point) _____ According to Burton, the reason that middle and secondary teachers give grades is because school districts require it.

Sentence Completion

21. (1 point) _____ represents the grading standards that consists of pre-established percentage scores required for a given grade.

22. (1 point) _____ is the term used to represent the grading standards that rank students from highest to lowest, specifying what percentage of students will receive As, Bs, Cs, Ds, and Fs.

23. (1 point) _____ is the term that refers to establishing a standard of achievement in which all students who successfully meet the standard can receive the highest available grade.

24. (1 point) _____ is the term that refers to the number of units students complete in a given amount of time.

Short Answer/Essay

25. (4 points) List two principles that are important in report card grading.

_____
_____
_____
_____

SCORING	POINTS NEEDED FOR MASTERY	POINTS RECEIVED
I. WHAT ARE STANDARDIZED TESTS AND HOW ARE THEY USED?	9	_____
II. WHAT TYPES OF STANDARDIZED TESTS ARE GIVEN?	9	_____
III. HOW ARE STANDARDIZED TESTS INTERPRETED?	9	_____
IV. WHAT ARE SOME ISSUES CONCERNING STANDARDIZED AND CLASSROOM TESTING?	9	_____
V. HOW ARE GRADES DETERMINED?	9	_____

FOR YOUR INFORMATION

This section of the study guide includes suggestions for further study of the information you have not yet mastered. You will find information on: 1) typical responses to the SELF-CHECK item(s) from the text; and 2) key concepts, principles, and theories addressed in the text.

I. WHAT ARE STANDARDIZED TESTS AND HOW ARE THEY USED?

1. SELF-CHECK ITEM: What is the main difference between standardized and non-standardized tests? How are standardize test results used in student selection, placement, diagnosis, and evaluation? What is a minimum competency test and how does it hold teachers and schools accountable for what students learn?

TYPICAL RESPONSE: Discuss standardized test uses.

> Standardized tests are uniform in content, administration, and scoring in order to allow for the comparison of results beyond the confines of a particular classroom or school -- unlike non-standardized tests.

> Standardized tests are used in a variety of ways. First, standardized tests are often used to select students for entry or placement in specific programs (e.g., SATs or ACTs) or to decide which students to place in specific academic tracks (e.g., college preparatory or vocational). Standardized tests are also used to diagnose learning problems or strengths and to determine modes of remediation. Another use of standardized tests is to evaluate the progress of students in particular areas such as math or reading. And, standardized tests can contribute to improving the academic process by holding schools accountable.

2. KEY CONCEPTS, PRINCIPLES, AND THEORIES.

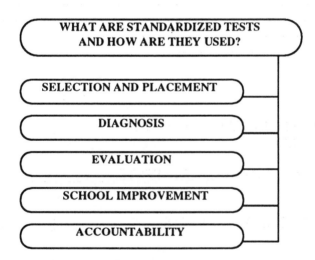

WHAT ARE STANDARDIZED TESTS
AND HOW ARE THEY USED?

SELECTION AND PLACEMENT

DIAGNOSIS

EVALUATION

SCHOOL IMPROVEMENT

ACCOUNTABILITY

II. WHAT TYPES OF STANDARDIZED TESTS ARE GIVEN?

1. SELF-CHECK ITEM: Define *aptitude test* and *achievement test* and describe how each is measured. What is the difference between a norm-referenced achievement test and a criterion-referenced achievement test? Give an example of an appropriate use for each type of test.

TYPICAL RESPONSE: Compare and contrast aptitude and achievement tests (norm- and criterion-referenced).

Aptitude tests are designed to predict the ability of a student to learn or perform particular types of tasks. The most widely used measures of aptitude are intelligence tests and multi-factor aptitude tests. Achievement tests, in contrast, are designed to diagnose student difficulties and to measure formative and summative learning. Common achievement tests include achievement batteries, diagnostic tests, and subject area achievement tests.

Aptitude and achievement tests are measured using either norm-referencing or criterion-referencing. Norm-referenced measures compare a single score to all other scores using percentiles. They are most appropriate when comparisons of this type are needed. Criterion-referenced measures compare a single score, often presented as raw scores, number correct, or percents, to a well-defined set of objectives.

Criterion-referenced and norm-referenced measures differ in a number of ways. Criterion-referenced tests take the form of a survey battery, a diagnostic test, or a single subject test. In contrast to norm-referenced tests that are designed for use by schools with varying curricula, criterion-referenced tests are often constructed around a well-defined set of objectives. Criterion-referenced tests also differ from norm-referenced tests in that measurement often focuses on student performance with regard to specific objectives rather than on the test as a whole. Finally, criterion-referenced tests differ from other achievement tests in the way they are scored and how the results are interpreted. There is usually a score for each objective.

2. KEY CONCEPTS, PRINCIPLES, AND THEORIES

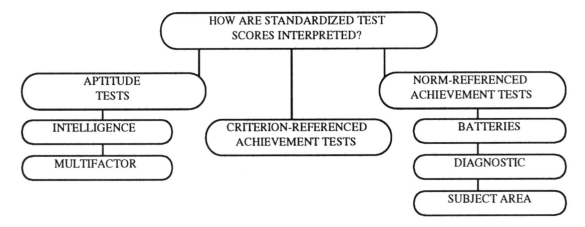

III. HOW ARE STANDARDIZED TEST SCORES INTERPRETED?

1. **SELF-CHECK ITEM:** Describe how standardized test percentile scores, grade-equivalent scores, and standard scores are derived and interpreted.

TYPICAL RESPONSE: Describe percentiles, grade equivalent scores, and standard scores.

Percentiles indicate the percentage of students in the norming group who scored lower than a particular score. For example, students who achieved the median (i.e., 50% scored above and 50% scored below) for the norming group would have a percentile rank of 50 because their scores exceeded those of 50 percent of the students normed in the group.

Grade equivalent scores relate students' scores to the average score obtained by students at a particular grade level. In theory, the score of 5.5 would represent five years, five months; however, grade equivalent scores should be interpreted cautiously. For example, a fifth grade student who scores 7.5 on a measure of math ability is by no means ready for seventh grade math.

Standard scores describe test results according to their place on the normal (bell-shaped) curve. A normal curve describes a distribution of scores in which most fall near the mean, with a smaller number of scores moving away from the mean. One important concept related to normal distribution is the standard deviation, which is a measure of the dispersion of scores. The standard deviation is the average amount that scores differ, or spread out, from the mean.

2. KEY CONCEPTS, PRINCIPLES, AND THEORIES

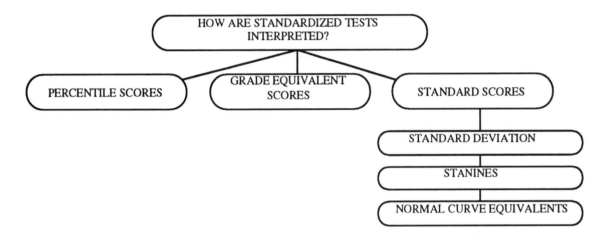

IV. WHAT ARE SOME ISSUES CONCERNING STANDARDIZED AND CLASSROOM TESTS?

1. SELF-CHECK ITEM: Define *validity* and *reliability*. What criticisms of standardized tests relate to issues of validity and reliability?

TYPICAL RESPONSE: Define and discuss validity and reliability.

Validity is the degree to which a test is appropriate for its intended use. Reliability is the consistency of test scores obtained from the same student at different times.

Issues surrounding standardized testing are strongly debated by educators. While they are intended to yield valid and reliable results, several drawbacks exist. One is that they give false information about the status of learning in the nation's schools. The "Lake Wobegon Effect" (note: Lake Wobegon is a fictitious town where "all the men are strong, the women good looking, and the children above average.") demonstrates this. In theory, 50 percent of standardized test scores should fall below the mean and 50 percent should be above. This is not true for several reasons. First, schools, under pressure from the public to produce above average scores, "teach to the test." Also, administrators have been known to "select" high achieving students to take some tests such as the pre-SAT so that overall scores are high. While highly unethical, this procedure makes the school look good; however, some students who could use the practice on the pre-SAT are not given the opportunity to take the test.

2. KEY CONCEPTS, PRINCIPLES, AND THEORIES

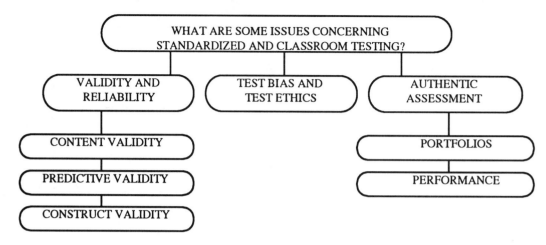

V. HOW ARE GRADES DETERMINED?

1. SELF-CHECK ITEM: Describe the advantages and disadvantages of letter grades, absolute grading standards, grading on the curve, contract grading, and mastery grading.

TYPICAL RESPONSE: Outline advantages and disadvantages of various grading systems.

TYPE OF GRADING	ADVANTAGES	DISADVANTAGES
no grades	non-threatening	students perform better under graded systems
letter grades	set by individual teachers, set by school administration	teachers can use extremes; either too easy or too difficult
absolute grading standards	criteria for achievement set prior to instruction	students' scores dependent upon difficulty of outcome
relative grading standards	place students' scores in relation to others in group	grades are not representative of achievement in schools using tracking; creates competition among students; artificial boundaries
mastery grading	grades are temporary; allows for correction	progress in relationship to group is eliminated
continuous progress grading	measure of skill progression	progress in relationship to group is eliminated

2. KEY CONCEPTS, PRINCIPLES, AND THEORIES

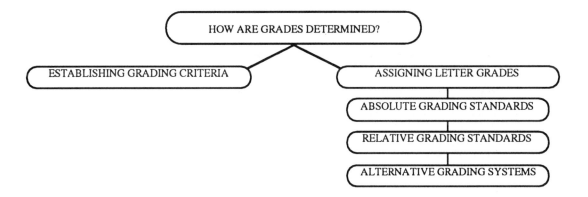

FOR YOUR ENJOYMENT

This section of the study guide includes suggestions for enriching your understanding of a chapter heading you have mastered. You will find information on activities related to the headings and suggestions for research papers, interviews, or presentations.

I. WHAT ARE STANDARDIZED TESTS AND HOW ARE THEY USED?

1. Interview a special education teacher or school psychologist about the types of standardized tests used to assess student performance. Ask how the results are used.

2. Discuss the ethics of holding schools accountable for achievement as determined by standardized test results. Include in your discussion ways that administrators and teachers can raise overall test scores without raising overall achievement.

II. WHAT TYPES OF STANDARDIZED TESTS ARE GIVEN?

1. For a research topic, review the literature on standardized testing.

III. HOW ARE STANDARDIZED TEST SCORES INTERPRETED?

1. Interview a special education teacher or school psychologist about the interpretation of standardized tests. How do they report grades to teachers, administrators, parents, and students?

IV. WHAT ARE SOME ISSUES CONCERNING STANDARDIZED AND CLASSROOM TESTING?

1. Discuss issues related to standardized testing and bias.

2. Discuss issues related to authentic assessment.

V. HOW ARE GRADES DETERMINED?

1. Discuss the advantages and disadvantages to: 1) grading on effort; 2) grading on attendance; 3) grading on improvement; and 4) grading on participation.

CHAPTER FOURTEEN: SELF-ASSESSMENT

DIRECTIONS: Below are questions related to the main ideas presented in the chapter. Correct answers or typical responses can be found at the end of the study guide.

1. What are the advantages and disadvantages of minimum competency testing?

2. Which of the following types of standardized tests is designed to predict future performance?

   A. placement test
   B. achievement test
   C. aptitude test
   D. diagnostic test

3. Currently intelligence is measured as a

   A. ratio of chronological age to mental age.
   B. percentile.
   C. mean of 100 and a standard deviation of 15.
   D. percentage of items correct on an IQ test.

4. Which of the following interpretations would apply to a sixth-grade student who has scored at the mean on a standardized test?

   A. percentile = 90; stanine = 9; $z = 20$
   B. NCE = 50; $z = 0$; percentile = 50
   C. GE = 7.2; stanine = 5; NCE = 45
   D. $z = 1$; NCE = 60; percentile = 50

5. Two classes of math students average 75 on a test, but the students in one class have scores that are much more spread out; this means their results will have a larger

   A. mean.
   B. median.
   C. standard deviation.
   D. normal curve.

6. A seventh-grader has a grade-equivalent score of 9.4 on a standardized test. Which of the following interpretations can be made from these results?

   A. The student is ready for ninth grade work.
   B. The test was too easy and should be renormed.
   C. The student has done as well as an average ninth-grader.
   D. The student scored at the 9.4 percentile.

7. Which of the following terms refers to a measure of a consistency of test results over multiple applications?

    A. predictive validity
    B. content validity
    C. construct validity
    D. reliability

8. Match each validity type with its description.

_____ a measure of the match between the test items and instruction given	A. construct validity
_____ a measure of the ability of a test to forecast behaviors	B. predictive validity
_____ a measure of the degree to which test scores reflect its intention	C. content validity

9. What are the major criticisms of standardized tests?

10. What are the advantages and disadvantages of absolute grading standards and relative grading standards?

PRACTICE TEST ANSWERS

1. Selection and placement, diagnosis, evaluation, improvement, and accountability

2. A, B, C; aptitude test, norm-referenced achievement test, criterion referenced achievement test

3. Intelligence tests and multifactor aptitude tests

4. Achievement batteries, diagnostic tests, and subject area achievement tests

5. Criterion referenced achievement tests differ from norm-referenced achievement tests in that they are constructed around well-defined objectives, measured by assessing the number of objectives or "skills" met, and use a cutoff score.

6. Derived scores

7. Percentile scores

8. Grade equivalent scores

9. A; Standard deviation

10. C; Bell-shaped curve

11. C; With a mean of 100 and a standard deviation of 15

12. Stanine scores are standard scores that have a mean of five and a standard deviation of two. Each stanine is reported as a whole number and represents .5 standard deviations.

13. Normal curve equivalents can range from 1 to 99, with a mean of 50 and a standard deviation of approximately 21. NCE scores are like percentiles except that the intervals between the scores are equal.

14. True; Valid test results are a measure of the student's knowledge of some content area.

15. True; Reliable results are consistently accurate.

16. C, B, A; Construct validity evidence, predictive validity evidence, content validity evidence

17. Multiple choice standardized tests give false information about a school's status, are unfair to some groups of students; corrupt process of teaching and learning, and attend to simple, easily tested skills

18. Portfolios or performance assessments

19. False; Primary teachers give grades because it is school policy.

20. False; Middle and secondary teachers give grades to inform students.

21. Absolute grading

22. Relative grading

23. Mastery grading

24. Continuous progress grading

25. Grades should never be a surprise to students and grades should be private.

SELF-ASSESSMENT ANSWERS   Chapter 1

1. Intentional teachers do things on purpose. They are critical thinkers who are able to problem solve and transform information from educational psychology into sound classroom practices.

2. Principles explain relationships between factors, such as the Premack Principle. Laws are simply principles that have been thoroughly tested and found to apply in a wide variety of situations, such as Thorndike's Law of Effect. Theories are sets of related principles and laws that explain broad aspects of learning, behavior, and other areas of interest such as Piaget's theory of cognitive development.

3. a, c, b. Laboratory experiments have highly controlled conditions and internal validity. Randomized field experiments are conducted under realistic conditions involving frequent assessments over time. Single-case studies make observations of a single individual or group over time.

4. b, a, d, c. Descriptive researchers simply seek to describe something of interest. Randomized field experiment researchers test practical treatments under realistic conditions. With correlational studies, the researcher studies variables as they are to see if they are related. Laboratory experiments exert a very high degree of control over all variables at the cost of relevance.

5. a. Experimental researchers create special treatments, then analyze the effects.

6. c. A negative correlation means that one variable increases (class rank) as a second variable decreases (absences).

7. c. Ethnography involves observation of a social setting over an extended period of time.

8. Subject matter involves what is taught (content). Pedagogy involves how subject matter is taught (teaching strategy or technique).

9. Making the right decisions depends on the context within which the problem arises, the objectives the teacher has in mind, and many other factors, all of which must be assessed in the light of common sense.

10. Educational psychology is the accumulated knowledge, wisdom, and seat-of-the-pants theory that every teacher should possess to solve in an intelligent fashion the daily problems of teaching.

SELF-ASSESSMENT ANSWERS   Chapter 2

1. b. Two central issues have been debated for decades among developmental psychologists. One relates to the degree to which development is affected by experience (nature vs. nurture) and the other relates to the question of whether development proceeds in stages (continuous vs. discontinuous).

2. a, c, d, b. During the sensorimotor stage (birth to age two), babies and infants explore

their world by using their senses and motor skills. Hypothetical and abstract thought are characteristics of formal operational learners. Preoperational children have difficulties when attempting to solve conservation tasks. Inferable reality, seriation, and transitivity are characteristics of the concrete operational learner.

3. Assimilation is the ability to interpret new experiences in relation to existing schemes. When old ways of dealing with the world simply do not work, a learner modifies an existing scheme (accommodation).

4. c. Researchers have found that young children could solve conservation problems when the task was presented in a simple way with familiar language.

5. c. Studies show that learners who use private speech learn tasks more effectively than do other learners. Vygotsky suggested that teachers encourage learners to use private speech and that teachers use scaffolding, problem solving, and assisted discovery.

6. b. Concrete operational learners are approximately ages seven to eleven. Erikson notes that individuals who are six to twelve are in the stage of industry vs. inferiority.

7. a. Erikson viewed adolescence as a time when individuals work on issues of identity.

8. b, c, a. Self-chosen, ethical principles guide the moral behavior of postconventional decision makers. Preconventional individuals are concerned with the self. Conventional individuals are concerned with the wishes and rules of the group.

9. Hoffman's theory of moral development complements the work of Piaget and Kohlberg by acknowledging the role of cognitive abilities and reasoning skills in explaining moral behavior. His theory differs from the stage theories by considering the role of motivation and parenting practices on moral behavior. Hoffman argues that empathic distress, or experiencing the suffering of others, is a powerful motivator of moral choices and helping behaviors.

10. Preoperational children are learning to use symbols to represent the objects in their world; however, their thinking remains egocentric and centered. At the same time, they are working on issues of initiative and base their moral reasoning on avoidance of punishment and personal gain. Concrete operational learners have developed the ability to decenter, conserve, reverse thought, classify, categorize, and sequence. At the same time, they focus on the demands of acquiring new academic and social competencies and behave in ways that meet the conventions of the group. Formal operational learners think about non-existent possibilities, hypothesize, and reason in logical ways. At the same time, they are working on issues of identity and use conventional moral reasoning.

SELF-ASSESSMENT ANSWERS   Chapter 3

1. a. The major physical accomplishment for preschoolers is increased control over the large and small muscles.

2. a. Psychologists generally agree that play is an important part of kindergarten, needs to be more emphasized, and contributes to cognitive training.

3. b. A main driving force behind participation in compensatory preschool programs is that it increases disadvantaged children's readiness skills for kindergarten and first grade.

4. b. By the end of the preschool years, children can use and understand an almost infinite number of sentences, hold conversations, and know about written language.

5. b. Preoperational thought is that stage at which children learn mentally to represent things. This occurs between the ages of two and seven.

6. a. During middle childhood, peers become more important.

7. b. Individuals in a state of foreclosure have never experienced an identity crisis. They have made occupational and ideological commitments, but these commitments reflect their parents' beliefs.

8. d. Factors that lead to dropping out of school include school failure, retention, assignment to special education and poor attendance.

9. c, b, a, c, a, a, b. Oral language, prosocial behavior, and sociodramatic play occur during early childhood; friendships and conflict management first occur during middle childhood and preadolescence; intimacy and identity diffusion occur during adolescence.

10. Child development has important implications for classroom instruction at each grade level.

I. Early childhood classroom instruction
    A. Cognitive and language development
        1. Language acquisition and development
        2. Reading
        3. Writing
    B. Socioemotional development
        1. Peer relationships
    C. Instruction examples
        1. Encourage involvement with print
        2. Encourage group work and play
II. Middle childhood and preadolescence classroom instruction
    A. Cognitive development
        1. Concrete thinking
    B. Socioemotional development
        1. Growing importance of peers
    C. Instruction examples
        1. Provide experiences that are grounded in the concrete and the familiar
        2. Encourage dialogues that explore values, attitudes, peer acceptance
III. Adolescence classroom instruction
    A. Cognitive development
        1. Abstract thinking
    B. Socioemotional development
        1. Opposite-sex relationships
        2. Identity development
    C. Instruction examples
        1. Provide opportunities that call for hypothetical-deductive thought
        2. Encourage adolescents to explore roles

SELF-ASSESSMENT ANSWERS   Chapter 4

1. b. Sociologists define social class, or socioeconomic status (SES), in terms of an individual's income, occupation, education, and prestige in society; not by race.

2. b. The term "working class" is used to refer to families whose wage-earners have relatively stable occupations not requiring higher education.

3. a. As socioeconomic status increases, so do standardized test scores.

4. While behavior differences may be greater within groups than between them, research shows that gesturing and touching patterns as well as the use of humor and joking influence the ways in which students approach learning tasks.

5. c. Projections forecast that by 2026, 25 percent of all students will come from homes in which the primary language is not English.

6. b. Referendums, such as California's Proposition 227, limit the amount of time that students may receive assistance in learning English.

7. Multicultural education is not a single program, but a philosophy. Modifications in the curriculum, adaptations of instruction, and changes in the communication of attitudes and expectations in the area of socioeconomic status, race, ethnicity, religion, culture, language, gender, intelligence, and learning styles all contribute to the celebrations of diversity.

8. c. Feingold has argued that males are more variable than females in quantitative reasoning, which means that there are more very high-achieving males and more very low-achieving males than there are females in either category.

9. b. Males receive more disapproval and blame from their teachers than females do, but also engage in more interactions with their teachers in such areas as approval, instruction giving, and being listened to.

10. Intelligence can be defined as a general aptitude for learning or an ability to acquire and use knowledge or skills. Binet saw intelligence as a single score or intelligence quotient set at 100 for average (50th percentile). Spearman claimed that while there are variations in ability from task to task, there is a general intelligence factor (g) that exists across all learning situations. Sternberg described three types of intellectual ability: intelligence, wisdom, and creativity. Guilford proposed 180 types of intelligences—six of mental operations times five of contents times six of products. Gardner lists eight intelligences: linguistic, musical, spatial, logical-mathematical, bodily-kinesthetic, knowledge of self, understanding of others, and naturalistic.

SELF-ASSESSMENT ANSWERS   Chapter 5

1. d. Feeling anxious when a teacher announces a test is a learned response. This reaction may be unconscious or involuntary, but it is learned nonetheless. The student associates the test with less than enjoyable circumstances over which she or he has little control.

2. c, b, d, a. Ivan Pavlov conditioned dogs to react to a conditioned stimulus (classical conditioning). Edward Thorndike stated that an act that is followed by a favorable effect is likely to be repeated in similar situations; an act that is followed by an unfavorable effect is not likely to be repeated (Law of Effect). B.F. Skinner used consequences to control behaviors (operant conditioning). Bandura studied how learning occurs by imitating or observing others.

3. a. Primary reinforcers satisfy basic human needs. Some examples are food, water, security, warmth, and sex.

4. The Premack principles states that activities less desired by learners can be increased by linking them to more desired activities. Two examples of the Premack principle include: 1) giving students computer game time when their work is finished; and 2) extending recess time if students' behavior is exemplary prior to recess.

5. a. Positive reinforcers are pleasurable consequences that serve to increase behaviors.

6. a. Attention, retention, reproduction, and motivation are observational learning phases.

7. c. Vicarious learning is observing the consequence of others' behavior (social learning theory). Meichenbaum's model for cognitive behavior modification centers on the individual asking himself or herself questions such as "What is my problem? What is my plan? How did I do?"

8. c. Behavioral theories of learning limit the study of animals to their observable and measurable behaviors.

9. Punishments, like reprimands or loss of privileges, do not work well with students, according to behavioral theorists. Most classroom behaviors can be managed through the use of reinforcers. This requires paying attention to desired behaviors and ignoring (unless safety is an issue) inappropriate ones. Many teachers use punishment because, whether we like it or not, it is a part of our schools, communities, and value system.

10. Classical condition is the pairing of a neutral stimulus with an unconditioned stimulus to produce a conditioned response. Operant conditioning is the use of consequences (reinforcers and punishers) to control the occurrence of behaviors.

SELF-ASSESSMENT ANSWERS   Chapter 6

1. d. The sensory register is the component of the memory system where information is received and held for very short periods of time. It has two important educational implications. First, people must pay attention to information if they are to retain it. Second, it takes time to bring all the information seen in a moment into consciousness.

2. b, c, a. The storage system in which memories of experiences can be stored is episodic memory. The component in which enormous amounts of general information can be stored is semantic memory. The type of memory associated with automaticity is procedural memory.

3. a. Retroactive inhibition is a form of interference caused when learning new, but

similar to previously learned, information; therefore, avoid teaching the new information in a way that is consistent with the method used to teach the previously learned information.

4. Automaticity refers to processing of information that is so rapid and easy that it takes little or no mental effort. It is primarily gained by practice far beyond the amount needed to establish information or skills in long term memory. For example, think of a young girl who is learning to play a certain piece of music on the piano. She begins slowly, painfully, and sometimes erroneously, memorizing each note. She may have to use a mnemonic strategy to remember the notes. During this first stage, she will need to look at the notes written on the sheet music, determine what each note is, one at a time, and then, search for the corresponding key on the piano. As she works with the piece of music for many, many hours, she puts notes together (compilization). For example, a measure of "play C, play E, play G" now becomes "play CEG". Then individual measures are compiled into larger and larger pieces. Once she can successfully play the piece, the knowledge of the notes and the corresponding actions (finger movements on the piano) are fused. She automatically plays the piece, no longer thinking about notes or keys; she just plays the music.

6. b, c, a. Paired-associate learning tasks involve learning to respond with one member of a pair when given the other member of the pair (states and capitals). Serial learning involves learning a list of terms in a particular order (order of the planets). Free-recall learning tasks involve memorizing a list, but not in any specific order (major organs).

7. a. Outlining presents the main points to the material in a hierarchical format while mapping identifies connections between main ideas.

8. c. Advance organizers are activities and techniques that orient students to the material before reading or class presentations.

9. Teachers can make learning relevant to students by activating their prior knowledge in several ways including the use of advance organizers, analogies, and elaboration.

10. Material that is well organized is much easier to learn and remember than material that is poorly organized. Hierarchical organization, in which specific issues are grouped under more general topics, seems particularly helpful for student understanding. Questions and diagrams presented before the introduction of the instructional material can also help students learn.

SELF-ASSESSMENT ANSWERS   Chapter 7

1. b. Learner control does not describe effective instruction. The other strategies listed demonstrate the interaction between the student and the teacher.

2. g, f, c, b, e, a, d. The seven steps in a direct instruction lesson would be in the following order: g) State learning objective and orient students to lesson; f) review prerequisites; c) present new material; b) conduct learning probes; e) provide independent practice; a) assess performance and provide feedback; d) provide distributed practice and review.

3. a. During the "present new material" phase of direct instruction, the teacher teaches the lesson, giving examples, demonstrating concepts, and so on.

4. Strategies that make independent practice time effective include: 1) do not assign independent practice until you are sure students can do it; 2) keep independent practice assignments short; 3) give clear instructions; 4) get students started, and then avoid interruptions; 5) monitor independent work; and 6) collect independent work and include it in student grades.

5. d. Direct instruction methods do not work well in the teaching of critical thinking skills, according to the research. Direct instruction is particularly appropriate in teaching a well-defined body of information or skills that all students must master. It is less appropriate when exploration, discovery, and open-ended objectives are the object of instruction.

6. It is clear that direct instruction methods can improve the teaching of certain basic skills, but it is equally clear that much is yet to be learned about how and for what purposes they should be used. The prescriptions derived from studies of effective teachers cannot be uncritically applied in the classroom and expected to make a substantial difference in student achievement. Structured, systematic instructional programs based on these prescriptions can markedly improve student achievement in basic skills, but it is important to remember that the research on direct instruction has mostly focused on basic reading and mathematics, usually in the elementary grades. For other subjects and at other grade levels we have less of a basis for believing that direct instruction methods will improve student learning.

7. a. Research indicates that low achievers should have as much time to respond as high achievers. Research has also found that teachers tend to give up too rapidly on students whom they perceive to be low achievers and not give them the same amount of wait time.

8. b. Transfer of learning is the application of knowledge acquired in one situation to new situations. For example, students having a knowledge of geometry should be better prepared to solve a perspectives problem in art.

9. d. Questions with one answer or with simple answers are not appropriate for group discussions.

10. During a whole-class discussion, teachers play the role of moderator. They guide the discussion and help the class avoid dead ends while ideas are drawn from students. Rules about how to deal with students who are quiet, or who talk too much, argue, or interrupt, should be determined and explained to students before the discussion begins.

SELF-ASSESSMENT ANSWERS   Chapter 8

1. a. The constructivist revolution draws heavily on the work of Piaget and Vygotsky, both of whom emphasized that cognitive change takes place only when previous conceptions go through a process of disequilibration in light of new information.

2. c. In mediated learning the teacher guides instruction so that students will master and internalize the skills that permit higher cognitive functioning.

3. c. Constructivist approaches to teaching emphasize top-down rather than bottom-up instruction. The term top-down means that students begin with complex problems to solve

and then work out or discover the basic skills required.

4. Scaffolding provides support for learning and problem solving, which could include clues, reminders, encouragement, breaking the problem down into steps, or providing an example.

5. d. Research suggests that cooperative learning programs are not effective where students are grouped together by ability. Mixed-ability grouping seems to have better results.

6. b, a, c. Learning together involves students working in four- or five-member heterogeneous groups on assignments. The groups hand in a single completed assignment and receive praise and rewards based on the group product. In Jigsaw, students are assigned to six-member teams to work on academic material that has been broken down into sections. Each team member studies her or his section. Next, members of different teams who have studied the same sections meet in expert groups to discuss their sections. Then the students return to their teams and take turns teaching their teammates about their sections. Group investigation is a general classroom organization plan in which students work in small groups using cooperative inquiry, group discussion, and cooperative planning and projects.

7. c. Research comparing cooperative learning to traditional teaching methods have consistently favored cooperative learning as long as two essential conditions are met. First, some kind of recognition or small reward must be provided to groups that do well so that group members can see that it is in their interest to help their group-mates learn. Second, there must be individual accountability.

8. The role of a teacher in a discovery lesson is that of facilitator. The teacher can teach in ways that make information meaningful and relevant to students, by giving them opportunities to discover or apply ideas themselves, and by teaching students to be aware of and consciously use their own strategies for learning. A disadvantage of discovery learning might be that some ideas are to be "discovered", leaving some students with fragmented knowledge or misconceptions.

9. c. Functional fixedness is a block to solving problems that is caused by an inability to see new uses for familiar objects or ideas.

10. Students can be taught several well-researched strategies to use in solving problems such as: 1) identify problems and opportunities; 2) define goals and represent the problem; 3) explore possible strategies; 4) anticipate outcomes and act; and 5) look back and learn.

SELF-AWARENESS ANSWERS   Chapter 9

1. a. The QAIT model of instruction includes quality of instruction, appropriate levels of instruction, incentive, and time.

2. a, b, c, d. Aptitude means that students have the prerequisite skills necessary to understand new information. Understanding instruction is the degree to which the teacher monitors how well students are learning. Perseverance refers to the students' level of motivation. Quality of instruction refers to the set of activities that make up teaching.

3. d. Mastery learning allows learning time to vary while keeping the level of achievement consistent. This provides for student differences. The basic idea behind mastery learning is to make sure that all students have learned a particular skill to a pre-established level of mastery before moving on to the next skill.

4. a. Norm-referenced tests that compare students to each other are not central features of mastery learning. In mastery learning the goal is to have the student compete with himself or herself in terms of mastery of the material.

5. d. Untracking focuses on having students in mixed-ability groups and holding them to high standards while providing many ways to reach those standards.

6. Within-class ability grouping is a system of accommodating student differences by dividing a class of students into two or more ability groups for instruction in certain subjects. Between-class ability grouping is the practice of grouping students by ability level in separate classes.

7. b. Research evaluating the effects of peer tutoring on student achievement has generally found that this strategy increases the achievement of both tutees and tutors.

8. b. The term programmed instruction refers to individualized instruction methods in which students work on self-instructional materials at their own levels and rates.

9. c. There is little research on the achievement outcomes of Internet involvement, and there is criticism that the Internet is a costly frill that can allow corporate interests to further penetrate schools.

10. b. Compensatory education programs, Title I, and early intervention programs are designed to assist students placed at risk.

9. Traditional classrooms can impede the use of mastery learning because they are based on time (the amount of information a student can learn during a unit, a quarter, a semester, a year) rather than the learning itself (learning all the information, regardless of the time it takes).

10. One factor that would make a peer tutoring program effective would be to use high school students as tutors for middle school students. A second factor would be to adequately train and monitor the tutors.

SELF-ASSESSMENT AWARENESS   Chapter 10

1. d. physiological; e. safety; b. belongingness and love; g. self-esteem; c. need to know and understand; a. aesthetic; f. self-actualization.

2. b, c, a. Behavioral theory suggests that motivation is a product of reinforcement. Attribution theory connects successes and failures to ability, effort, task difficulty, or luck. Expectancy theory states that success is tied to probability and incentive to succeed.

3. Skinner would say that the student is motivated to get good grades because she or he has been or wants to be rewarded for doing so. Maslow would say that the student is motivated to get good grades because he or she has an underlying need to know and understand the world.

4. c. A student with an internal locus of control is one who believes that success or failure is due to her or his own efforts or abilities.

5. b. Ability and effort attributions are internal to the individual. Although task difficulty is essentially a stable characteristic, the teacher wants the students to try harder regardless of ability level or task difficulty. Luck is unstable and unpredictable.

6. b. A student who tends to choose either very easy or very hard tasks would most likely be avoiding failure. When students succeed, they like to believe that it is because they are smart, not because they are lucky or because the task is easy. Students who fail believe they have bad luck, which allows for the possibility of succeeding next time.

7. a. Students who are motivationally oriented toward learning goals would be more interested in taking a challenging course. Their interest in the topic becomes a driving force because of the opportunity to make themselves more knowledgeable regardless of the difficulty of the material.

8. c. The main idea underlying the Individual Learning Expectations (ILE) model is grading on the basis of improvement. With the ILE model students are recognized for doing better than they have done in the past, for steadily increasing performance until they are producing excellent work all the time.

9. b, c, a. In a cooperative goal structure, one student's hard work increases the others' chances of success. If students are in competition, any student's success means another's failure. In an individualized goal structure, one individual's success or failure has no consequence for others.

10. Grading on improvement might tell students who have not done well in the past to feel they still have an opportunity to be successful; however, grading on improvement might be an inaccurate representation of what students actually know. Additionally, it hurts high achieving students because they have less room to improve.

SELF-ASSESSMENT ANSWERS   Chapter 11

1 a. Classroom management includes strategies for preventing and responding to misbehavior.

2. c. Engaged time, or time on-task (the number of minutes actually spent learning), is the measure that most frequently is found to contribute to learning.

3. a. Engaged time is time on-task.

4. c, b, d, a. Withitness describes teachers' actions that indicate awareness of students' behavior at all times. Group alerting refers to questioning strategies that are designed to keep all students on their toes during a lecture or discussion. Overlapping refers to the teacher's ability to attend to interruptions or behavior problems while continuing a lesson or other instructional activity. Accountability is the degree to which people are held responsible for their task performances or decision outcomes.

5. d. Class rules do not need to be created by the students and teacher together.

6. a, prevent misbehaviors; c, use nonverbal cues; e, praise appropriate behaviors; d, use verbal reminders; and b, apply consequence

7. d, identify target behavior and its reinforcer(s); b, establish a baseline for the target behavior; a, select and use reinforcers and, if necessary, punishers; c, phase out reinforcement

8. c. Behavioral learning theory suggests that teachers use programs and strategies based on observation of correct behavior and rewards.

9. Research first suggests that teachers should use reinforcers to increase desired behaviors rather than punishers to decrease undesired ones. Punishers should only be used as the last option and should involve a loss of privilege(s), but never physical punishment.

10. Speaking out of turn is a minor infraction and should be ignored or stopped with a soft reprimand. Teasing another student might best be handled by speaking privately with the teaser. Modeling and praising of appropriate relationship behaviors would help. Shoving another student on the playground is a serious safety issues that calls for intervention.

SELF-ASSESSMENT ANSWERS   Chapter 12

1. The terms handicap and disability are not interchangeable. A disability is a functional limitation a person has that interferes with her or his physical or cognitive abilities. A handicap is a condition imposed on a person with disabilities by society, the physical environment, or the person's attitude.

2. a. Approximately 1.2 percent of all students ages 6 to 17 have mental retardation.

3. b, c, d, a. Language disorders are impairments in the ability to understand language or to express ideas in one's native language. Learning disabilities are associated with learning problems that are not predicted by an individual's IQ. Speech disorders include articulation (or phonological) disorders such as omissions, distortions, or substitutions of sounds. Emotional and behavioral disorders are characterized by problems with learning, interpersonal relationships, and control of feelings and behavior.

4. a. Sensory impairments are problems with the ability to receive information through the body's senses.

5. acceleration and enrichment. Acceleration programs offer rapid promotion through advanced studies for students who are gifted or talented. Enrichment programs present assignments or activities that are designed to broaden or deepen the knowledge of students who master classroom lessons quickly.

6. b, c, a, d. Public Law 94-142 requires special education services to eligible students. Public Law 99-457 extends the entitlement to free, appropriate education to children ages three to five. Public Law 101-476 requires that schools plan for the transition of adolescents with disabilities into further education or employment starting at age 16. Public Law 105-17 raises educational expectations for those with disabilities and increases the role of parents in the education of their children.

7. 1. general education classroom; 2. resource room; 3. part-time mainstreaming; 4. self-contained special education classroom

8. 1. referral for evaluation; 2. placement; 3. testing and assessment; 4. signed parental approval of the IEP

9. Effective teaching of mainstreamed students with special needs in general education classrooms involves cooperative learning, computerized instruction, buddy systems, peer tutoring, consultation with special education specialists, and team teaching.

10. Tests used to determine eligibility for special services may not be appropriate for students who belong to a minority group. Minority group students are overrepresented in impoverished groups, which might mean they come from communities that cannot afford adequate educational facilities and programs.

SELF-ASSESSMENT ANSWERS   Chapter 13

1. c. An instructional objective, sometimes called a behavioral objective, is a statement of skills or concepts that students are expected to know at the end of some period of instruction.

2. The performance is to *locate*, the condition is *given a map*, and the criteria is 100 percent (i.e., *all*).

3. Analysis objectives involve having students see the underlying structure of complex information or ideas.

4. c. A behavior content matrix is a chart that classifies lesson objectives according to cognitive level. Using a behavior content matrix in setting objectives forces one to consider objectives above the knowledge and comprehension levels.

5. Evaluations provide students with feedback about their work, assist teachers in making instructional decisions, inform parents as to how their child is doing, provide information for selection into certain programs, assure accountability, and provide incentives for achievement.

6. d. According to Gronlund, each type of achievement test has its own requirement, which must fit the particular use that will be made of the results.

7. b, a. Summative evaluations follow instruction and evaluate knowledge or skills. Formative evaluations are administered during units of instruction and measure progress or guide the content and pace of lessons.

8. Parents are capable of understanding both norm-referenced and criterion-referenced grading. Parents of young children often see their students assessed according to achievement of skills. Parents of older children and adolescents often look for comparisons of the son or daughter with others, especially on standardized tests.

9. a. The purpose of devising a table of specifications in testing is to indicate the types of learning to be assessed for different instructional objectives.

10. Both objective and subjective assessments of student work are useful in making educational decisions; however, research about the reliability of portfolio assessment is disappointing because different raters have given very different evaluations on the same portfolio.

SELF-ASSESSMENT ANSWERS   Chapter 14

1. Minimum competency tests focus on important skills students are expected to have mastered to qualify for promotion. Advantages of minimum accountability testing include: 1) it increases the pressure on schools and teachers to pay attention to students who might otherwise be overlooked. Another advantage is that accountability encourages schools to search out improved instructional methods and guarantees routine evaluation of any innovation they try. However, the accountability movement has its critics. Many argue that minimum competency testing focuses schools on minimums rather than maximums. Others are concerned that schools will teach only what is tested. Many educators point out that accountability assessments fail to take into account differences among students. A school or classroom may test low because the students are from disadvantaged backgrounds rather than because they were given poor instruction. High-stakes testing can lead schools and districts to adopt policies that artificially inflate scores.

2. c. Aptitude tests are designed to predict future performance. It is meant to predict the ability of students to learn or perform particular types of tasks rather than to measure how much the students have already learned.

3. c. Over the years the chronological age/mental age comparison has been dropped, and IQ is not defined as having a mean of 100 and a standard deviation of 15. Most scores fall near the mean, with small numbers of scores extending well above and below the mean.

4. b. The national mean on the standardized test is 50 and the percentile of the student's reported score is 50. A z-score mean is set at zero.

5. c. Standard deviation is a statistical measure of the degree of dispersion in a distribution of scores.

6. c. It can be assumed that the student has scored as well on the test as the average ninth-grader, the equivalent of 9.4, which may be interpreted as ninth grade, fourth month.

7. d. Reliability is a measure of the consistency of test scores obtained from the same student at different times.

8. c, b, a. Content validity is a measure of the match between the content of a test and the content of the instruction that preceded it. Predictive validity is a measure of the ability of a test to predict future behavior. Construct validity is the degree to which test scores reflect what the test is intended to measure.

9. Critics argue that standardized tests 1) give false information about the status of learning in the nation's schools; 2) are unfair (or biased against) some students; 3) tend to

corrupt the process of teaching and learning; and 4) focus time, energy, and attention on the simpler skills that are easily tested.

10. Absolute grading provides teachers considerable leeway in assigning grades but scores may depend on the difficulty of the test given. Relative grading is based on how well other students performed on the same test. An advantage is that it places a student's score in relation to others, without regard for the difficulty of a particular test; however, students in a class of high achievers must get much higher scores to earn an A or B than students in a class of lower achievers.

NOTES

NOTES

NOTES

NOTES

NOTES

NOTES

NOTES

NOTES

NOTES

NOTES

NOTES